The Art of Bassoon Playing

by William Spencer
Revised by Frederick A. Mueller

Summy-Birchard Inc.
exclusively distributed by
Warner Bros. Publications Inc.
15800 N.W. 48th Avenue
Miami, Florida 33014

Table of Contents

List of Illustrations

Illustrations No. 1, 3, 4, and 25 courtesy of Fox Products Corp., So. Whitley, Ind.

Introduction

The place of the bassoon in the orchestra, band, and especially in the small woodwind ensemble is an important one. It has expressive qualities and tonal colors possessed by no other instrument. In spite of its relatively high cost, its intrinsic value to these organizations is worth the expenditure of funds and the time necessary to develop proficient players. One accepts the tone color produced by the professional ensembles; yet in many potentially fine amateur community orchestras and school ensembles, the bassoon is either misused, poorly played, or not used at all because of a lack of knowledge concerning certain aspects of the bassoon on the part of the instrumental teacher. Since the performance of much of the better orchestral and small ensemble music is dependent upon a bassoonist with an adequately developed tone and technical facility to manage the more difficult passages encountered, the instrumental teacher needs to have more than just an elementary knowledge of the bassoon.

The need for a reference on the advanced teaching problems of the bassoon has long been expressed by students and teachers of the bassoon in both the public schools and colleges. Professional bassoonists and teachers who have made the bassoon their major instrument are usually to be found only in large metropolitan areas and in a few large universities and conservatories. Therefore, opportunities for the student and for the future instrumental teacher to study with a bassoon specialist are limited.

Although the problems of general interpretation and over-all development of musicianship can be dealt with by a fine musician and teacher, regardless of his performing medium, there are nevertheless many details and problems related to teaching and playing the bassoon that require special attention and knowledge. Since the opportunity for individual study with a bassoon specialist is limited, it was felt that a reference of teaching aids and suggestions such as those used by professional bassoonists would be of value. Although there is some information to be found in periodicals and method books about the various problems of bassoon playing and teaching, these materials are not generally available when needed. The teachers of instrumental music have a

tremendous task in learning the very best of teaching methods for every instrument. This is in itself quite an undertaking, but the teacher must also be able to suggest suitable solo and study literature for the student. Even the teachers who are professional bassoonists have a need for a knowledge of a wider variety of solo literature which they can assign to students on various levels of achievement. Many teachers do not have the time, the opportunity, or the knowledge to examine and select from the available literature suitable solo materials to meet the needs of their students in contests, programs, recitals, and for study. Evidence of this can be seen by an examination of recital programs and the music being played in high school contests. Although there are those who feel the bassoon is strictly an ensemble instrument, the writer feels that the study and performance of solos is one of the best means of encouraging an adequate study of the instrument. The practice of using a large amount of etudes and concocted exercises instead of good music should be discouraged.

The purpose of this book is to help meet the above needs by: (1) furnishing for the teacher of the high school and college bassoonist such teaching aids and information as will assist him to know the instrument better, to understand its problems, and to be able to deal with the student's performance problems with more understanding; (2) furnishing a guide for the selection of suitable methods, books and solo material for contests, recitals, and study, with suggestions and aids to assist the student to adequately perform the literature available.

The teaching aids offered are organized under four main headings: the instrument, the reed, production of bassoon tone, and articulation. The problems of each factor are taken up individually, with suggestions of solutions which have been used successfully by many fine teachers. These problems are those that most often appear in remedial work with students in high schools and colleges.

The methods, books and solo literature have been selected with the following criteria in mind: (1) to show the wide variety of music available; (2) to offer a selection of music suitable for various levels of ability and for various occasions; (3) to present only music originally written for the bassoon; and (4) to include examples of music that are worthwhile in themselves and interesting to study and perform.

The information and teaching suggestions, for the most part, have been gathered and compiled by the writer over a period of years as a result of experiences gained by playing the bassoon professionally and teaching in elementary schools, high schools and college. Information gained through study with two noted professional bassoonists and teachers (Hugo Fox, Chicago Symphony Orchestra and Simon Kovar, New York City), notes taken at clinics and lectures, interviews and study with many other performers and teachers of voice and wind instruments have also been used.

William G. Spencer

Preface to the Revised Edition

In revising Mr. Spencer's excellent discussions, it has been my aim to bring to the reader's attention the many changes that have recently occurred in bassoon playing, pedagogy, and manufacture. Several bassoon manufacturers and artist-teachers of the bassoon, including Don Christlieb, Alan Fox, Jack Linton, Jr., William Polisi, Dr. Eugene Rousseau of Indiana University, and Dr. William Bigham of Morehead State University have contributed their help to this project. My special thanks to Jean Wiggins and Joseph Martin of Morehead State University for preparing the bibliography and discography.

F. A. Mueller

PART I

The Instrument

Many of the problems that beginning or fairly advanced bassoonists have can be traced to a poorly made instrument or to one that is in bad repair. Much of the remedial work done in more advanced lessons is a result of undesirable playing habits picked up by the students in attempting to play on such instruments. Teachers everywhere will agree that instruments of fine quality are not only more conducive to fine playing results, but are of exceeding value to the proper progress of the student's musicianship. However, even a casual survey of the bassoons used in the schools leads one to wonder that there are even as many bassoonists coming along as there are. This condition is caused by: (1) the high cost of good bassoons, (2) the relatively poor quality of medium-priced bassoons, (3) the lack of knowledge and experience in choosing a suitable instrument, and (4) a general neglect of the proper care and adjustment of the instrument. Since very little can be done about the cost or quality of the instruments that are available, it remains for the teacher or the student, if he is buying his own instrument, to choose more intelligently. After he has selected a bassoon, the care it receives and the adjustments made will determine how well it will play and how long it will last.

By far the most widely-used bassoon in the schools today is the German or Heckel system bassoon. This is true in the symphonies also, although many years ago the French or Conservatory system bassoon was in general use. This was probably due to the fact that most of the woodwind players in the early development of the symphony orchestras in this country came from France. The French bassoon is by no means outdated, since it is still used in many countries, including France,

Spain, Italy, and in the military bands in England. The teacher will not have to concern himself with the French bassoon for the most part except to be able to recognize it. (See Illust. 1.) He may encounter one which was purchased many years ago in a school system or one which was purchased by mistake. Although the bassoons look somewhat similar, there are a great many easily discernible differences. Perhaps the most outstanding one is the number and the arrangement of the keys. The German bassoon has a great many more keys, particularly on the boot joint. Although it has been said that one could tell the difference by the ring and the color of the instrument, this is no longer true. The German bassoon was traditionally made with an ivory ring and a mahogany finish, while the French bassoon used a metal ring and was stained ebony. In recent years, some professional bassoonists have had German bassoons made with a metal ring and stained ebony. There are, of course, many other differences; the size of the bore, the quality of the sound, the fingering system, the shape of the bell, and the type of reed used. (For a more detailed discussion of the German and French reeds, see Part II.)

Among those who are not bassoonists, there has often been some misunderstanding as to the use of the name "Heckel" in connection with the German bassoon. One hears and reads of the "Heckel system bassoon" and of the "Heckel bassoon" without realizing that they may not be the same thing. The German bassoon had its beginning when Carl Almenraeder and J. A. Heckel entered into a partnership in 1831. Since that time, the German bassoon has been developed to its present form in the Heckel factory and bassoons made by the Heckel family have been recognized the world over as the finest available.

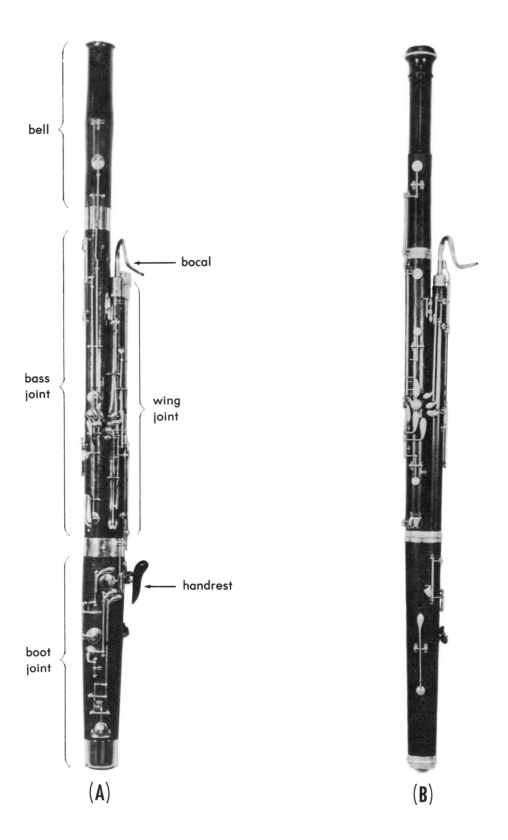

bell

bocal

bass
joint

wing
joint

handrest

boot
joint

(A)

(B)

ILLUSTRATION 1

A comparison of a German (A) and a French (B) bassoon

Chronological Developments Leading to
the Heckel System Bassoon

No. of Keys	Maker or Manufacturer	Locale or Country	Date
2-10	Christoff Weigel	Nürnberg, Germany	ca. 1698
9-11	Savary père	Paris	ca. 1788-1826 [1]
6	John Parker	London, England	ca. 1795
8	Martin Lempp	Vienna, Austria	ca. 1810
12	Johann Mollenhauer	Fulda, Germany	ca. 1830
13	Unknown		
14	Joh. Sam. Stengel	Bayreuth, Germany	ca. 1810-1857
14 [2]	Carl August Schaufler	Stuttgart, Germany	ca. 1850 [3]
15	Adler & Joh. August Heckel	Biebrich/Rhein, Germany	ca. 1824-1827
15-16	Karl Almenraeder	Biebrich/Rhein, Germany	1841 [4]
17-19	Unknown	France	1839
20	Chromatic scale (BB-flat to d″)	France	1850
21	August Heckel added the "piano" or "whisper" key	Biebrich/Rhein, Germany	1912
21-24	Wilhelm Heckel Company, Franz Groffy, Dir. (the latter, famous Heckel bassoon maker and engineer)	Biebrich/Rhein, Germany	to present

Range

CC, DD, etc.   C, D, etc.   c, d, etc.   c′, d′, etc.   c″, d″, e″

The bassoon has lagged behind the flute and the clarinet in technological development as well as in methods of teaching and performance. Before World War II students of bassoon were dependent on European builders and performer-teachers, and the Almenraeder 1840 vintage instrument was still being used as the model for bassoon construction. Since the late 1940's, American bassoon players have been primarily responsible for refining the old nineteenth-century Heckel system, first in performance, and later in methods of manufacture.

Today the principal bassoon manufacturers who export instruments to the United States are Heckel, Mollenhauer, Puechner, Schreiber, Moennig, and Riedel. Bassoonists Lewis Hugh Cooper and William Polisi of the United States have undertaken to alter imported European bassoons for American performers, contributing refinements in key mechanisms, guards, and tuning devices. To Don Christlieb, Paul Lehman, Alan Fox, and Jack Linton belong the credit for refining the acoustical properties of the bassoon. American manufacturers who have incorporated these modern innovations in their instruments include Hugo and Alan Fox, Jack Linton and Son, the late Jack Aman, and Hans Moennig. We owe all these individuals a debt, for without their dedication and creative work,

---

[1] Lyndesay G. Langwill, "The Development of the Bassoon after 1750," in *The Bassoon and the Contrabassoon* (New York, W.W. Norton & Co., Inc., 1964), p. 59.

[2] The 6-keyed through 14-keyed bassoons may be seen in the Yale University Collection of Musical Instruments.

[3] Richard Rephman, *Yale Collection of Musical Instruments* (New Haven, Yale University, 1968), p. 11 and insert between pp. 14 and 15.

[4] Karl Almenraeder's (1786-1843) *School of Bassoon Playing* was intended for the 15-keyed bassoon. See Blume, "Fagott," in MGG, Vol. 3 (Kassel, Bärenreiter-Verlag, 1954), p. 1729.

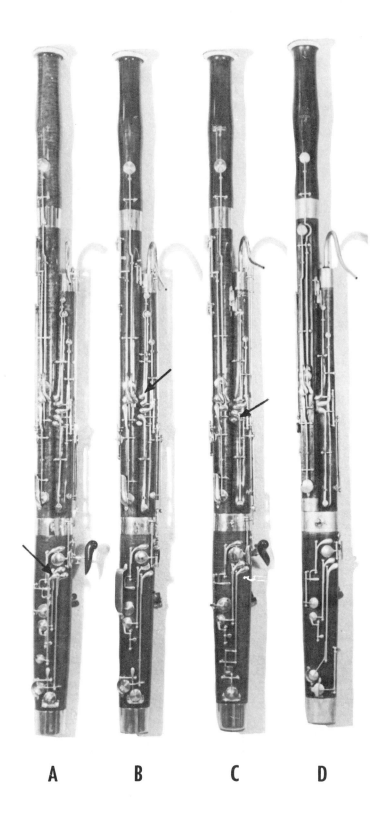

ILLUSTRATION 2

Four Heckel system bassoons

    A) Twenty-four keyed bassoon (D key plus A♭-B♭ trill)

    B) Twenty-three keyed bassoon (added high D key)

    C) Twenty-two keyed bassoon (standard, crook key added)

    D) Twenty-one keyed bassoon (old)

the art of bassoon playing would never have become so highly developed.

Teachers and students who work with the bassoon should know something of the materials used in the construction of the Heckel system bassoon. Most bassoons today are made from hard maple. Although other woods have been used, such as rosewood and sycamore, they have been found to be inferior to maple. According to the manufacturers, maple works easier, takes a better finish, and will better resist cracking. It is also lighter in weight and therefore easier on the player. The outside of the instrument is stained either mahogany or ebony and finished with several coats of lacquer. As with furniture finishes, the more expensive instruments will have a much finer and better-lasting finish than the less expensive ones. The color of the stain is purely a matter of individual taste. Some professionals seem to prefer the ebony, although the mahogany color is more traditional. The inside of the bore is ordinarily treated with oil to prevent moisture from entering the pores of the wood. Some manufacturers have impregnated the wood with a special substance (other than oil) which makes it water-resistant. Bassoons treated in this manner do not have to be oiled. The wing joint and the small side of the boot joint have been lined with hard rubber or ebonite. This practice has become almost universal with the German bassoon today, and only very old bassoons will be found lacking this rubber lining.

Plastic materials have been successfully employed in bassoon manufacture because of their ability to withstand extreme changes of temperature and humidity. Some of the plastics used by bassoon makers are polypropylene, lintonite, and fiberglass.

Plastic bassoons are popular for beginning students from elementary to high school age. Linton and Fox have even constructed smaller than standard-size instruments as well as beginning models fitted with fewer keys.

The metal parts of the bassoon may be made of nickel silver, German silver, or brass. "Investment" or "precision" casting, which provides for one-piece keyed mountings, has been in use since 1947. Many innovations in key plating and forging refinements have been designed to withstand acidity from the palms of the hands and finger tips, hand and finger pressure on keys and levers, and variations in temperature due to gas heating elements, open flame heaters, and pilot lights of kitchen appliances.

The traditional ivory ring at the end of the bell serves not only a decorative purpose, but also protects the wood against cracking or chipping. As was previously stated, this ivory ring is sometimes replaced by a metal ring like that found on the French bassoon, but this is strictly a matter of individual preference and will only be found occasionally. In many cases, the ivory is being replaced by plastics, especially on less expensive bassoons. The material used and the workmanship indicated in the finish of the bell and the ring are often a good indication of the quality of workmanship in the entire instrument. For this reason it is important to pay particular attention to an otherwise quite unimportant detail.

Selecting the Bassoon

Whenever possible, a professional bassoonist should assist in picking an instrument. Since this is not always possible, the following plan for becoming more proficient in judging bassoons is suggested:

One should begin by reading, asking questions of experts, and by examining and comparing instruments to recognize quality of materials, workmanship and musical qualities. He should then become acquainted with the various makes of bassoons and the reputation they have with professionals, students and schools.

One should take every opportunity to listen to, play on, and examine fine bassoons in order to know what good instruments are like. The best way to do this is to work with a professional bassoonist. This is particularly important if a teacher is working with students who have played or are playing on poor instruments. It has been found that the student who has played on one bassoon for a number of years will tend to take the playing characteristics of that particular instrument as a guide for all others. If the teacher is to be of value to the student, he will need to be able to distinguish whether the fault is with the instrument or with the student. If possible while working with the professional, he should be asked to play on the school bassoons. His comments should be noted carefully and compared with the ideas of the teacher.

Next, one should become acquainted with an experienced repairman and his views on the good and bad points of the bassoons he has worked on. Since repairmen work with all makes of instruments, they will be able to tell which bassoons stand up better through the years and what to look for in materials and in workmanship.

The actual selection of the bassoon can be divided into two phases: (1) the objective test (visual inspection of the instrument), and (2) the playing test.

The Objective Test

Features to look for in selecting an instrument might include:
1. Heckel system: 21 to 24 keys.
2. Automatic "piano" (or "whisper") key.
3. F-sharp trill key on wing joint.
4. Rollers to serve both thumb positions and their respective keys, as well as the little

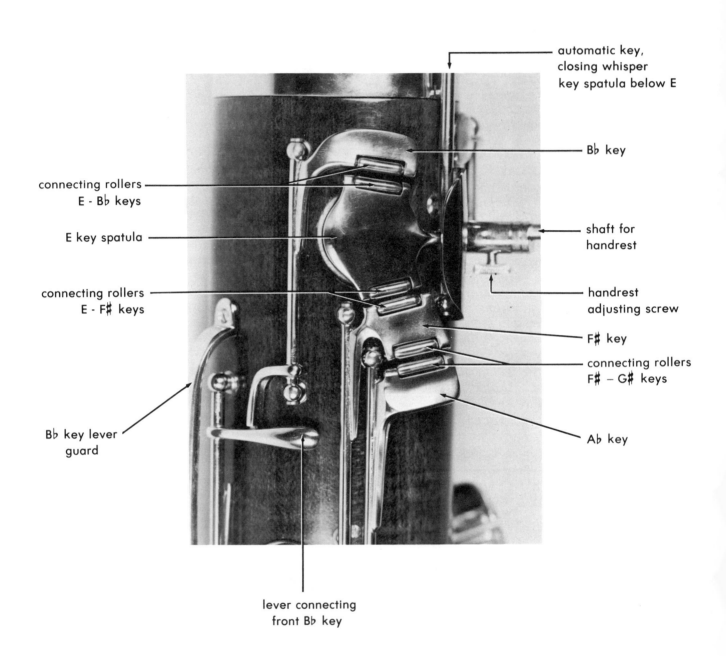

automatic key,
closing whisper
key spatula below E

B♭ key

connecting rollers
E - B♭ keys

E key spatula

shaft for
handrest

connecting rollers
E - F♯ keys

handrest
adjusting screw

F♯ key

connecting rollers
F♯ – G♯ keys

B♭ key lever
guard

A♭ key

lever connecting
front B♭ key

ILLUSTRATION 3

Rear View: right thumb

finger keys. Rollers permit easy and rapid movement to and from keys of different size and shape.

5. Automatic ring key for g♯ with cork pads.
6. Guards for B-flat, D, E, and G spatulas.
7. Two silver-plated or plain brass bocals (numbers 1 and 2).

High quality bassoons will have many or all of the above features present or mounted. Accessories will include a sturdy case, straps (seat or neck), handrest, reed case, and cleaning rod.

Additional mechanisms. Although the above items are the minimum specifications for a standard Heckel system bassoon, these additions are most desirable:

1. Joint locks will assure proper alignment of all sections of the instrument when the inexperienced student player assembles his instrument.

2. The high D key is found on most contemporary model bassoons, but the high E speaker, or auxiliary key, will be found only on professional instruments.

3. The low extension to AA (below the fundamental B-flat) will require the extension of the bore, using a specially-constructed longer tube. Such an extension can be obtained on special order. With the use of this extension, however, the B-flat will not be able to sound.

4. The piano (or whisper) key locking mechanism will permit rapid and guaranteed response in leaps and rapid movement within and down to the low register, below and above E. Locks may be fitted on either the wing joint or the boot for operation with either left or right thumb.

5. An efficient trill from A-flat to B-flat can only be executed with the addition of a trill key—the A-flat—B-flat trill key. Few professional bassoonists use this particular trill key.

6. Posts with springs locked in position with a special screw. The post locks, which serve to keep the post from turning with the constant pressure of the spring, are an important consideration. As the instrument gets older and the wood begins to season, the posts tend to become loose due to the wood drawing away from the metal. If these locks are not used, the posts will turn with the pressure of the spring and bind the key. Old bassoons without locks are continually out of adjustment.

7. Wing joint equipped with metal linings in octave key holes.

8. Finger holes lined with nickel silver tubes that extend into the inside bore. In recent years the metal linings in the tone holes have been added to the better instruments as standard equipment. The linings keep water from running out of the holes and causing the "bubbling" which can sometimes ruin a solo passage. The metal lining in the octave key holes was found neces-

sary because these holes often closed up as the instrument aged. These holes are very small to begin with, and any water which runs into them will cause the wood to swell and thereby reduce the opening considerably.

9. C-sharp tone hole lined with hard rubber.
10. B hole in boot joint rubber lined.
11. Automatic G hole metal lined.
12. Extra octave key—the high D speaker key. This key is placed on the wing joint immediately above the C speaker key. (Illus. 25) It is operated by the left thumb and is used for (a) slurring up to D above the staff, and (b) as a speaker key above high C:

Ex. 1 (a)   (b)

13. A bar or guard over the B♭ and F♯ keys on the back of the boot joint. This is added to keep these keys from getting tangled in the player's clothing. If the seat strap method of suspending the bassoon is used, the instrument will rest against the leg at this point and often the B♭ and F♯ keys are kept from opening fully. This bar can be added quite easily by any repairman. (Illust. 4-C.)

14. Covered keys for the finger holes of the wing and boot joint. Although this arrangement is seldom seen, it has been included here so that the teacher and student of the bassoon will know of it. It is not recommended for the advanced bassoonist.

15. A half-hole key similar to the oboe first finger key. Since one of the most perplexing problems of playing the bassoon well is the use of the half-hole on the first hole of the wing joint, this device could very well help solve the problem. This would be especially useful for beginning players. It can be added by a bassoon repairman to any bassoon.

These mechanical improvements and additions have been included here so that the teacher will recognize them if they are encountered. Also, if he knows of these additions and their uses, he will be able to recommend them to the advanced bassoon student if the need should arise.

Continuing with the visual inspection of the bassoon, close attention should be directed to the quality of the workmanship. First, the finish of the wood will give a clue. The finer finishes will have a satiny look rather than a hard, glossy look. The finger holes will be smoothed out and finished at the edges. The inside of the bell, the bass joint, and the large side of the boot joint will be finished very smoothly and will be stained the same as the outside.

Second, the keys and metal trim should be examined. The key cups, spatulas, and rods will be finished smoothly without any sharp edges. The

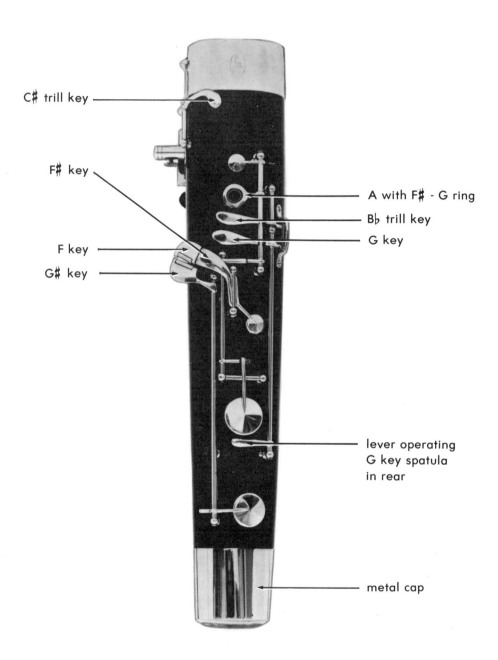

C# trill key

F# key

F key

G# key

A with F# - G ring

B♭ trill key

G key

lever operating
G key spatula
in rear

metal cap

ILLUSTRATION 4

Boot joint (front view)

spatulas will be arranged to fit the hand and adjusted for even height. The keys that need special attention in this respect are those operated by the thumbs and the right hand little finger. The ring keys provide an excellent test of just how carefully a bassoon has been manufactured, assembled, and regulated. The centering of the ring to the raised hole that it serves is important. Perfect centering is a mark of craftsmanship.

Third, it is often possible to get an indication of the quality of workmanship of the entire instrument by the kind of material used and the care exercised in making and assembling the ring on the end of the bell. Poor quality plastic substitutes for ivory and ill-fitting edges often indicate a poor quality of work in less conspicuous places.

Fourth, the joints should fit together snugly without undue tightness or looseness. The cork or thread should be applied smoothly and neatly.

The Playing Test

Having inspected the instrument or instruments in question to determine the quality of materials and the degree of craftsmanship indicated, one comes to the real test of the musical worth of the bassoon by playing it. Fortunately there is a high correlation between high quality of materials and craftsmanship and the musical qualities of an instrument. Granted that there are small individual differences between even fine bassoons, most players will agree that a superior bassoon has qualities that others seem to lack. It is for this reason that the student and the teacher are advised to become acquainted with a professional bassoonist's instrument. If one is to be able to recognize quality in an instrument, he must have had some first-hand experience with a quality instrument. These factors of quality are much the same as for other musical instruments: a rich resonant tone which is characteristic of the bassoon, an even and true intonation, a balanced scale, resistance to suit the performer, and a comfortable "feel" in the hands.

Since the condition of the instrument and the reed make so much difference in the way the bassoon responds, the person testing an instrument is cautioned to make sure that he has a good, reliable reed, that it fits on the bocal without leaking, and that the instrument has been checked for possible leaks. The following factors are to be considered during the playing test:

1. Tone quality. The tone should be full, resonant, and rich throughout the range of the bassoon. The player should be on the lookout for any exceptionally loud notes or soft notes. F♯ on the fourth line and G on the fourth space, for instance, are often bad from the standpoint of excessive resonance, even on good instruments. Notes in the low register that come from tone holes covered with a pad may be faulty due to a pad that is either too close to the hole or too far away. The upper register may be weak and uneven in tone quality. This may be due to the fingering combinations, but more often it is due to the bocal.

"By far the most singularly important part of the instrument, the bocal, dominates the response, resistance, and tone of the bassoon. It affects the overall pitch of the instrument as well as the relative intonation. . . . Even a mediocre bassoon may have reasonably good sound and scale if it is properly fitted with a good professional bocal."[1]

Heckel, Fox, and Kohlert make the most reputable and professional quality bocals. These differ in length from short to long: 00, 1, 2, 3, 4. The metals usually used are bronze, nickel plate, silver plate, and sterling silver. Silver-plated and brass (uncoated) bocals have least resistance. Some manufacturers have specific letter names regarding special bocal bores, bocal wall thicknesses, and apertures.

Good bocals are manufactured to tolerances measured in ten-thousandths of an inch. Thus, a small dent or a small particle may completely change the playing characteristics of the entire horn.[2]

The acoustics of the room in which the instrument is being played should be considered in testing for quality of tone. Either an exceptionally dead or live room will give a false impression. If at all possible, the bassoon should be tried in several different places or in a room in which the acoustics are known to be favorable for musical performance.

Since the actual tone of the instrument may sound different to the performer than to the listener, it is also advisable to have opinions from several different musicians.

2. Intonation. The bassoon should be tested and checked to tune to A-440 before it leaves the factory. If the bassoon being checked is flat with the Number 2 bocal, then the pitch can be raised a little by using the Number 1 bocal, since it is shorter than the Number 2. In some cases where it is necessary to raise the pitch above A-440, a Number O bocal can be obtained. Several other factors should also be taken into consideration when testing the intonation.

First, the reed can alter not only the individual notes but also the pitch of the entire instrument. Generally, the stiffer the reed the sharper the pitch; the softer the reed, the flatter the pitch. Also, very old reeds tend to go flat. The distance that the reed is placed on the bocal can also affect the pitch. The usual distance is about one-half inch. If the diameter of the bocal is smaller or larger than the one to which the reed has been fitted, it will be necessary

---

[1] Alan Fox, *Bocals* (South Whitley, Indiana, Fox Products Corp., 1969).
[2] Peter A. Figert, "Bassoon Rx," *Connchord*, Vol. 11, No. 3 (May, 1968), p. 21.

to fit the reed to the bocal properly before a valid intonation test can be made.

Second, the temperature should be considered. Musical instruments are ordinarily tested to tune to A-440 at 72° Fahrenheit with the instrument already warmed-up. The tester should take into consideration that a cooler or a warmer temperature will alter the pitch of the instrument. The cooler temperatures will lower the pitch and the warmer temperatures will raise the pitch.

Third, the tendency of the player to humor or "lip" various notes according to the way he hears them should be taken into consideration. This is certainly desirable in solo and ensemble playing, but when testing a new instrument this humoring of individual notes must be kept to a minimum. Even the best bassoons will need humoring, but an instrument that requires as little of this as possible is most desirable. A popular expression for playing without "lipping" or humoring individual tones is to play with a "dead-pan" embouchure. This will be difficult for the student to do at first, particularly if he has been playing on an instrument with bad intonation and does not realize that he has been humoring certain notes.

Fourth, various pitches may be altered by adjusting the position of the key spatulas or key cups over certain tone holes. For example, the pitch of both a and g may be lowered effectively by lowering the F and G spatula (front and rear of the boot joint).

The importance of having a competent bassoonist test the bassoon is emphasized when it comes to a question of intonation, since the experienced performer will know the tendencies of the various registers and particular notes. The upper register requires special attention because of the variety of fingerings available and used by different bassoonists. It should

be mentioned, however, that the variety of fingerings different from the standard ones recommended (see Illust. 24) have been developed to overcome intonation and tone quality deficiencies of individual instruments.

Don Christlieb of Christlieb Products was the first to discuss re-boring and changing the dimensions of the bore of the bassoon.[1] In order to improve bassoon intonation and response, Hugo and Alan Fox have altered the dimensions of the bore. Alan Fox has commented on the long and the short bore:

> The long bore bassoon was commonly produced by the Wilhelm Heckel Company from prior to World War I until the mid-twenties. It is suspected that they would still build it upon request, although it has not been encountered by this writer on any Heckel bassoons past the 6000 series (prior to 1930). (The Fox Bassoon Company has been building this type since 1951 and is still doing basic research on it, along with their efforts on the short bore model.)
>
> Its primary characteristics are a very even scale, in pitch and tone, octaves that play in tune with the fundamentals and with relatively firm pitch throughout the lower and middle registers. The sound is somewhat darker than that of its counterpart and it is pitched two or three vibrations per second lower. Depending on the reed employed (and to some degree, bocals), it can be tuned from A-437 to A-442.[2]

Alan Fox recommends the short bore instrument for professional players but says that beginning bassoonists will do better with the long bore instrument.

As a guide to the inexperienced teacher in checking the intonation of the bassoon, the following tendencies should be noted:

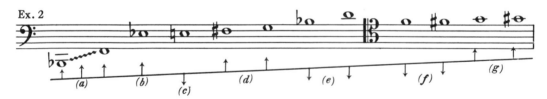

Ex. 2

(a) The notes from low B♭ to F tend to be sharp.

(b) E♭ tends to go sharp, especially if the reed is somewhat stiff.

(c) E and F have a tendency to be flat, especially if the reed is too soft.

(d) F♯ and G tend to be sharp in relation to the rest of the bassoon. The F♯ fingering with the right hand little finger is flatter and less resonant than the one fingered with the thumb.

(e) B♭ and D are usually bad for flatting.

(f) F and F♯ will usually be flat if played with the same lip and breath pressure as the surrounding

notes. A check of the fingering and the bocal should be made.

(g) G and G♯ have a tendency to be sharp on many bassoons. As in (f), the fingering and the bocal should be checked.

In testing for accuracy of intonation, one should play slowly. He should make use of major scales and chords in all keys. Intervals such as octaves, thirds, fourths, and fifths are also valuable.

[1] Don Christlieb, *Measuring the Conical Bore of the Bassoon, A Clinical Report,* Inter-American Music Bulletin No. 62 (Washington, D. C., Pan-American Union, 1967), 7 pp.

[2] Alan Fox, "Defining the Two Types of Bassoons—Long and Short Bore," *The Instrumentalist* (Nov. 1968), pp. 53-54.

If at all possible one should make use of one of the audio-visual aids now available, such as the Stroboconn or the newer Audio-Viewer. The use of these devices can make the basis for judgment much more objective.

3. Even scale. This factor is a combination of good intonation and an even tone quality. It is best tested by the playing of scales and passages which are characteristic of the bassoon in a rather slow tempo. Some indication of this quality can also be gained from playing scales at a rather fast tempo. At the faster tempo the player does not have time to adjust the lip to any discrepancies in pitch, and the true intonation of the individual notes will show up. It should be mentioned that by far the most important factor is tone quality, as small differences in pitch can be adjusted by a bassoon repairman.

4. Resistance. This quality has been described as "the capacity of the instrument to push back at the performer", or to give him something against which to exert his efforts. Although the reed is probably the most important factor in resistance, it has been found that even with the same reed different bassoons will vary in resistance. Nearly all performers will agree that this is an important factor, but they will vary in their individual tastes. The tester should be aware of the fact that an instrument that has even a slight leak anywhere will give a false impression of its resistance.

5. The "feel" of the instrument. The best-made bassoons have been designed to fit the hands and will feel comfortable. The keys will be placed for easy manipulation, and it will not be necessary to stretch the fingers or hands unduly to reach them. This is particularly true of the keys for the little finger and thumb of the right hand and for the left thumb. The key action on the artist bassoon will be light to the touch and the springs regulated for a balanced pressure within key groups operated by the same finger.

The actual inspection and playing test should take very little time, although it would seem like a lengthy procedure from the above description. It is suggested, however, that the final judgment of the instrument be held off until the bassoon has been tried several times. The high cost of any bassoon, whether it is a good one or not, makes it worthwhile to be certain one is getting his money's worth.

A good used bassoon is by far a better investment than an instrument of lesser quality even though it is new. The best source for such used instruments is the professional bassoonist. He will often have one himself, or he will know where a good one can be found. If one plans to choose a used instrument from another source, the same criteria used in picking a new instrument will apply, with these important additional checks:

1. Check the general condition of the wood, keys, and metal trim for signs of wear and deterioration. Although this will not interfere with the way the instrument performs, it should be considered in the price. The outside finish may be scratched or show excessive wear at the places where the hands come in contact with the wood. The tone holes should be checked for chipping and roughness. A careful inspection for cracks should be made. Signs of cracks or repaired cracks will usually be found near the ends of joints. If the bassoon has not been used for some time, the metal trim on the end of joints may be loose, which will probably indicate that the wood has become very dry. This in itself will not be detrimental, but if the bore is not treated with oil before the instrument is used a great deal, there is great danger of cracking.

2. Check the mechanical condition very carefully. This will include the pads, corks, and bumpers for hardness and wear; the keys for excessive end play; the springs for being either loose, broken, or rusty; the posts for looseness; the bocals for splitting, dents, and signs of having been bent.

3. Watch especially for signs of cracks and rotting wood in the bottom of the boot joint. Because excessive water collects here, this is the first place a bassoon begins to deteriorate. It will be necessary to remove the U joint for this inspection.

4. Cracks and checks in the surface of the hard rubber lining of the wing joint may indicate that water has leaked between the lining and the wood and has caused the wood to begin to rot. This will occur only rarely, in very old bassoons.

5. An instrument that is several years old may develop leaks in either the U joint or the insert in the upper end of the wing joint. These two possible sources of leaks should be checked very closely in addition to the regular inspection for leaky pads.

If the instrument being considered for purchase has a beautiful tone and good intonation but is in poor mechanical condition, it would be best to take it to a repairman for an appraisal. Even a complete overhaul including refinishing the wood and replating the keys is not too costly if the instrument is worth it musically.

When buying an instrument, whether new or used, it is well to keep in mind that the cost is a result of high quality materials and many hours of skilled labor. In spite of recent trends to standardize the making of musical instruments by the use of modern assembly line methods, the finest bassoons are those that are the result of individual artistry and craftsmanship. The very best bassoons cost more, but they are much more satisfying to play.

How to Check and Adjust the Mechanism of the Bassoon

It is important that the teacher not only become acquainted with the marks of artistic quality in bassoons as indicated by craftsmanship, choice of materials, and playing characteristics, but he needs to know more of what the mechanical condition of the instrument should be and how to keep it that way.

The bassoon, in spite of its large size in comparison to the other woodwinds, is really quite a delicate piece of equipment. Even with normal care and proper handling, the instrument can frequently get out of adjustment. Not all instrumentalists can or should do their own major repairing and adjusting, but they should learn to recognize a well-regulated mechanism and be able to make the small adjustments needed to keep it that way.

Elaborate equipment is not needed. The following tools and supplies will do very nicely:

1. A small screwdriver to match the size of the screws.

2. A small pair of pliers.

3. A spring hook. (A Number 9 crochet hook with a notch filed in the end will do.)

4. Small tweezers for picking up small screws or placing small pieces of cork between keys.

5. A sharp knife or razor blades.

6. An alcohol burner. (A match or cigarette lighter will do in an emergency.)

7. Glue. (Either a special cork and pad cement or a quick-drying cement will do.)

8. Cigarette paper, pieces of cork, felt, and leather. These items can be purchased at the hardware store, music store, or through a jewelry store. They can be stored along with the reed tools and equipment for care of the bassoon. A small fishing tackle box will be adequate and inexpensive.

Testing and Adjusting Procedures

Everything should now be ready to begin testing and, if necessary, adjusting.

1. All pads should seat perfectly, and the pad material should be soft and pliable.

A new instrument, or one that has been recently overhauled, will usually work perfectly for the first month or two. After that, some difficulty may be experienced in playing in the low register. One or two finger combinations may be found that do not sound right. This is often due to leaky pads. In order to find the pad or pads in question, one will save much time if he will play slowly down the chromatic scale from open F until a noticeable change in quality, intonation, or response is noticed. If it is possible, someone should tap or press the keys above this particular note while the instrument is being played.

The two easiest and most efficient tests for leaky pads are the air-pressure test and the feeler test. Testing can begin with the wing joint by holding the palm of one hand over the end, placing the other hand in position over the holes, and blowing into the other end. The bell and bass joint can be tested in a similar manner. The boot joint can be checked by holding the cheek over one opening while blowing in the other out of the side of the mouth, or a large cork can be used in one side. The right hand fingers will be in place on the holes and keys. The pads, if held down with normal playing pressure, should withstand considerable pressure. (The tendency to use more finger pressure than usual while testing for leaks must be guarded against.) If the least bit of air escapes anywhere, its location can be determined with the free hand or by blowing smoke into the joint. The smoke will leave a stain on the pad where it escapes. The search can usually be narrowed down to keys that are held down with a spring. Also to be suspected are pads which have become hardened because of water leakage. These will most often be found on the lower end of the boot joint.

If a small leak is found, the feeler test can be used next to make sure of the right pad. A strip of cigarette paper one quarter of an inch wide is cut to use as a feeler gauge. This paper is slipped under the pad, first one side and then the other, until all points around the pad have been checked. By holding the pad down with normal playing pressure and by pulling the paper out very slowly, one will be able to determine a leak by the lack of drag.

If a pad leaks on one side, a repair might be possible by tipping the pad toward that side. This can be done by heating the pad cup until the pad cement is soft and then moving the pad slightly over toward the leaking side. After the pad has been moved, the pad cup should be held down tightly until the cement cools. A recheck should then be made with the feeler gauge and air test. This process is continued until the pad has the same drag on all sides. If the pad is hard from age or from being water-soaked, it will be necessary to replace it entirely. It may be found that if the pad is held down by a spring, it is leaking because of a weak spring or binding post.

2. All connecting rods and bridge keys should be working perfectly without excessive play or noise.

Most connections between two keys, such as the low F and F♯ keys, are adjusted by means of cork or felt. As the instrument is played, these pieces of cork or felt tend to mat down or dent. This causes one of the keys to seat improperly. In addition to checking for leaky pads as before, one should go over the instrument very carefully by pressing the first key that causes two keys to close while tapping the second key lightly with the finger. If there is the slightest movement or sound, an adjustment is needed. This adjustment can be made by cutting a very thin slice of cork and gluing it over the old cork. Even a thin piece of paper will do in an emergency. The thickness will depend on the amount of play between the keys. Quick-drying airplane cement can be used in an emergency or a regular cork cement if there is more time. As a final check, the feeler gauge should be used.

The automatic mechanism that connects the piano key with the low E key usually requires special attention. The bridge key that extends from the wing joint to the boot joint will have either cork, leather, or felt used for silencing and adjusting. Care must be taken that this material is not torn off in assembling the instrument, but even with normal care it will wear down. Each time the instrument is assembled, this connection should be checked closely for proper alignment and operation. It has been found that a piece of leather or felt glued entirely around the bridge key will last the longest and will have less chance of being torn off.

3. All keys should work smoothly, quickly, quietly, and with a minimum of finger effort.

There are several factors which contribute to a finely adjusted key action. First, the springs need to be tensioned properly. There are two kinds of springs in terms of their action: those that hold keys down, and those that hold keys open. The springs that hold keys down need to be just strong enough to hold the key and pad down and keep it from leaking, but weak enough to be easily opened. The springs that hold keys open need to be only strong enough to return the key to the open position quickly after being depressed. The balancing of these springs should be done only by a competent repairman. This phase of key adjustment is most often neglected unless the bassoonist knows about it and insists upon its being done. Most often the spring tension is more than needed. This will be particularly true of those pads held down with a spring. If the pad is properly seated, it will not be necessary to have the spring so strong. Too strong a spring action can interfere with a smooth finger technique, especially if the keys involved are operated by the weaker fingers.

The second factor in smoothly operating keys is the problem of sticking pads. The first treatment for a sticking pad is to slip a piece of paper under the pad and, while holding the pad down, pull the paper out. This will usually remove any deposit or stickiness from the pad and tone hole. If the pad continues to stick after the paper has been tried several times, a piece of cloth lightly soaked with cleaning fluid can be used in the same manner. This will usually clean the pad, but if it does not, the key should be removed so that the pad can be more thoroughly cleaned and dried. The use of talcum powder is not recommended, as it will only cause further gumming if moisture comes in contact with the powder.

The third contributing factor to a smooth key action is clean and oiled bearings. One would not think that this would be a problem in this mechanical age, but most students neglect to clean and oil the keys of their instruments as they should. Periodic oiling of all key bearings with a high grade, non-gumming oil is a must. On the other hand, too much oil is bad, for it serves to catch lint and dust under and around the keys. A very small drop, such as can be gathered on the end of a toothpick or small screw driver, is sufficient. At least once a year the key rods and screws should be removed and the rods and the inside of the keys should be cleaned with a pipe cleaner. To avoid mixing up parts, remove the keys one at a time or one group at a time.

The repairing of loose posts and binding keys is a job for the repairman or for one who is experienced in making such repairs. Posts with springs attached cause the most trouble, and if the bassoon does not have post locks, they can be added at very little cost.

Finally, there are two minor adjustments which will make for more left thumb facility. The first is to bend the spatula for the piano key closer to and even in height with the C# key. This key is often too far away and either too high or too low to facilitate using the two keys together or for sliding from one to the other. The second adjustment is to move the small metal stop on the bass joint so that the keys on the wing joint are within a quarter of an inch of the keys on the bass joint. These keys may also have to be adjusted in height so that all of them are the same. It may be best to have a repairman make these adjustments unless the proper tools are available. These adjustments seldom need to be made on the very best bassoons.

4. All sources of leaks (other than the pads) must be sealed perfectly.

There are two such sources: the U shaped fitting at the bottom of the boot joint under the metal cap, and the ebonite insert at the top of the wing joint. Most bassoonists soon learn that the gasket between the removable U and the brass fitting on the bottom of the boot joint can leak and should be checked periodically. The best test is to close off the joint as in testing for a pad leak, dip the end of the bassoon in water up over the gasket joint, and blow air into the other end. Escaping air will form bubbles. To repair, one should put in a new rubber, cork, or leather gasket and dip it in melted wax before assembling. If the gasket is still good, it will only be necessary to renew the wax. Cork grease will sometimes do as well if wax is not available, but glue should not be used.

It is not as generally known that the joint between the brass fitting and the end of the wood can be the source of a leak. A leak here will usually not appear until the bassoon is several years old and has been used a great deal. Testing for this type of leak should be carried out in the same manner as above, but the end should be inserted in water to just below the first tone hole. The repair of this leak will have to be made by a competent bassoon repairman.

The second source of a leak not generally suspected is the insert at the top of the wing joint. This is the insert into which the bocal is fitted. Testing for this leak is done by adding the bocal to the wing joint leak test described before. If there is a leak, the insert can be reglued with wood glue.

5. The joint tendons should fit into the sockets smoothly and snugly.

If the wood was properly seasoned before the instrument was constructed, there will be little difficulty with ill-fitting joints. There will be some changes, however, caused by weather conditions and seasonal changes. A small amount of cork grease should be applied each time the bassoon is assembled. This is especially true of the bell and bass joints. These large joints are cumbersome and often difficult to put together and take apart unless cork grease is used every time. While some bassoons will have cork on the tendons, other may have thread. If a bassoon has cork, it will last much longer (if it is kept clean.) A small amount of cold cream should be applied, and then all old cork grease and dirt should be wiped off with a cloth. If the cork has become compressed and the joint is too loose, the cork should be swelled by first wetting it slightly and then applying heat with either a match or an alcohol burner. One must be careful not to burn the cork. If the wood swells and the joint becomes too tight, the cork should be sanded down with fine sandpaper. The thread-covered tendons can be adjusted by either taking off or adding some thread. A small amount of beeswax will help keep the loose ends of thread under control.

Occasionally the metal rings which serve to protect the ends of the joints become loose. It is not recommended that they be glued back. The usual procedure is to insert a thin piece of paper. The paper is laid over the end of the joint and then the ring is tapped on. After the ring is in place, the excess paper may be removed by wetting the edges and scraping with a fingernail or a dull knife.

Not all bassoonists will be able to make all of the small adjustments necessary to keep their instruments in top playing condition. However, they should certainly learn to recognize a well-regulated bassoon and to know when one needs adjusting. In many cases, musical or technical shortcomings of a player are actually due to faulty mechanical conditions of the instrument.

The Care of the Bassoon

Probably the most important factor contributing to the long life and continued usefulness of an instrument is proper daily care and handling. Most of the problems of small adjustments and even major repairs are the result of improper care, or in many cases, no care at all. The proper care and handling of an instrument should become a habit from the very beginning.

The daily procedures include the following:
1. Assembly and disassembly.
2. Correct carrying.
3. Drying the bore.
4. Wiping off the keys.
5. Drying wet pads.

Assembling the bassoon should be done in a careful and systematic manner. A very small bit of cork grease should be applied to the tendons each time the instrument is assembled, unless the joint becomes too loose. The wing and boot joints should be put together first, with special care with the pianissimo key automatic mechanism. The wing joint should be grasped in the left hand with the thumb in the curved out part and the boot joint in the right hand about in the middle. Care should be exercised not to apply undue pressure or strain to any posts or keys. Assembly of the instrument should be accomplished with a pushing, twisting motion, and the curved part of the wing joint should be lined up with the large hole for the bass joint. After assembly, one should lay this section in the case and put the bell and bass joints together. The bass joint can be held in the left hand and under the arm against the body for support while the bell is held in the right hand with the thumb pressing the B♭ key down. The joints should be pushed together with one twisting motion. Both sections can now be picked up; the boot joint and wing joint in the right hand and the bell and bass joint in the left. The bass joint should be slipped in place with a slight twist, being careful not to damage the keys. The final adjustments for the joint lock should be made according to the type of lock used. Finally, the bocal is put in. Be careful to grasp it near the large end. One should never attempt to put the bocal in or take it out by grasping it at the small end. If the bassoon is to be carried any distance, the bocal should not be left in the bassoon. Most accidents with the bocal occur while it is being carried in the instrument. When carrying the bassoon, one should grasp it by both the wing and bass joints at one time.

The instrument should be taken apart in exact reverse order. First, the bocal should be removed, the water blown out, finger prints wiped off, and the bocal returned to the case. As each section is taken apart, it should be laid in its place in the case before cleaning. The bassoon or parts of it should not be put on a chair or any other place where it may be knocked off and damaged.

After the instrument is taken apart, the wing joint and the boot joint should be swabbed out. The wool swabs usually furnished with the bassoon are very unsatisfactory for this purpose since they do not dry the bore and they tend to leave lint in the tone holes. A cleaning rod such as that used for cleaning guns, with a piece of cloth inserted in the eye and wrapped around the rod, works very well. Another method is to use a piece of chamois skin cut in the shape of a triangle, with the widest end no wider than four inches. If the chamois is wider than four inches, it may stick in the wing joint. A piece of stout cord with a weight attached is tied to the small end of the chamois skin. To dry the wing joint, one may pull the swab through two or three times. To dry the boot joint, one should lay the chamois out over the hole and, using one of the wool swabs, push the chamois down to the U in the bottom. The cord and the wool swab handle should then be grasped and pulled out at the same time. This is the most effective method of drying the bore at the lower end of the boot joint, where most of the moisture collects. It will not be necessary to swab out the bass and bell joints each time since very little, if any, moisture collects there. Any moisture that has collected in the finger holes should be blown out at the same time the bore is being dried.

After the inside of the bassoon has been swabbed out, the outside should be wiped clean of perspiration and finger prints to protect the finish of the metal and wood. A soft cloth or chamois skin can be kept in the case for this purpose. Much of the pitting and tarnishing of the metal can be discouraged by this procedure. As a result, the instrument will not only look better but the keys will feel smoother to the fingers.

Any pads which have become water-soaked because of water running out of the tone holes should be dried with either a piece of plain paper or a blotter. The pads on the lower end of the boot joint are most apt to be wet. Although the life of the pad will be extended to some degree by this procedure, it will be necessary to examine the pads closely for signs of hardening. The pads to watch especially are the low G and the two G♯ keys, as these holes collect the most water. Many bassoonists remove the bass joint and pour water out of the boot joint during the playing period. Since laying the instrument across the lap during rests will often cause water to run out of the holes, it is best to hold the instrument up at all times.

When putting the instrument in the case, one should never lock the bass and wing joints together with the joint lock. If these joints are fastened together and the case is dropped or receives a hard bump, the lock may be torn loose from the wood. This lock is only to be used when the instrument is assembled.

The weekly procedures include the following additional steps:
1. Washing the bocal.
2. Dusting under the keys.
The bocal needs to be washed out with warm water and soap at least once a week. The use of a very small brush, pipe cleaners fastened together, or a commercial bocal cleaner will help remove any deposits of food particles not removed by running water through the bocal. The small hole for the piano key should be cleaned out occasionally with a small broom fiber. A pin or a needle should not be used, as they might enlarge the size of the hole.

A small paint brush is best for dusting under the keys. If this dust and lint is allowed to collect over a period of time, it will interfere with the smooth operation of the keys.

Monthly care procedures are:
1. Oiling the key mechanism.
2. Polishing the wood, keys, and trim.
3. Cleaning out the finger holes.
4. Oiling the wood bore every six months.

All the key bearings should be oiled once a month if the bassoon is in daily use. An excessive use of oil will cause gumming and collect lint under and around the keys. A very small drop, such as will cling to the end of a small screw driver, is sufficient at each bearing point. A high grade, non-gumming oil such as is used in watches and clocks is the best.

The outside finish of the instrument will last much longer and will look better if it is cleaned and polished each month. A small amount of furniture polish or wax applied to the areas coming in contact with the hands will help preserve the finish. The keys and trim can be polished with one of the commercial polishing cloths. A paste or liquid polish should never be used on the keys, since it will get into the bearings and cause gumming. It may be used on the metal rings and guards, if necessary, to remove any excess tarnish.

The holes that the fingers usually cover on the wing and boot joints may need cleaning at this time. A toothpick, a piece of clarinet reed, or a pipe cleaner may be used to remove the grease and dirt. It will be best not to use any sharp metal object that may damage the hole. A small amount of bore oil should then be applied with a pipe cleaner. Any excess wear or chipping of the finish around these holes can be touched up with clear fingernail polish.

The bore of the large side of the boot joint should be oiled lightly about every six months. A special bore oil for this purpose can be purchased. For oiling, one should use an old swab or a piece of cloth over one of the regular wool swabs that come with the instrument. The oil should be used very sparingly. The usual procedure is to apply the oil to the cloth and wring out any excess oil before swabbing the bore. To protect the pads, one should place pieces of paper under them before oiling. The instrument should not be used for two or three days before or after oiling. This rest period will allow any moisture in the wood to evaporate before oiling and will also allow the oil to penetrate the wood before more moisture is introduced into the bore.

The joints lined with rubber need not be oiled. The bass and bell joints will need oiling only about once a year, if at all. However, these joints should be dusted out about once a month to keep them clean. Some makes of bassoons do not need any oiling of the bore at all, since the wood has been specially treated at the factory to prevent the penetration of moisture. If one is in doubt, it would be advisable to consult the dealer or the manufacturer. In the case of a new bassoon, the oiling procedure outlined by the factory should be followed. The procedure outlined above is only for bassoons that have been in use for more than a year.

The yearly check-up will include the following:
1. Checking all pads, springs, corks and general condition.
2. Cleaning and oiling the key mechanism.
3. Checking the U joint for signs of a leak.
4. Repadding or overhauling (every two or three years).

Many bassoonists take their instruments to the repairman for this yearly check, since he is experienced and has the equipment necessary for any repairs or adjustments that will have to be made. If the daily, weekly, and monthly procedures have been faithfully carried out, there will be very little to be done at this time. An instrument that has been properly taken care of will not only remain in top playing condition, but will be less expensive to operate.

The bassoon should be protected from excessive temperature changes. A case cover will be of value in this respect, as well as protecting the outside appearance of the case. If the instrument is very cold, it should be warmed up slowly; any quick change may cause the wood to split. It is advisable to open the case to allow the bassoon to reach room temperature before playing. Storage near radiators or in very dry rooms is dangerous. If small cracks in the wood do appear, they should be repaired immediately to keep them from opening up any farther. Small cracks on the outside of the instrument will not impair the playing condition so long as they do not extend to the inside or go through a tone hole. Cracks that have gone all the way through to the inside will require the services of an expert repairman.

In areas where excess humidity is a problem, the pads and keys will deteriorate very rapidly because of too much moisture.

Suspending the Bassoon

Playing progress can often be hindered by the way the bassoon is held while playing. Whether the performer is playing in a standing or sitting position, the bassoon should be held so that the player is looking over the bocal at the music. The instrument should not be held in a straight-up-and-down position. The left arm will fall close to the body, while the right arm and elbow should be held slightly up so that the wrist will not be cramped.

The traditional method of suspending the bassoon is by a neck strap. This is the only practical method for the standing position. If the neck strap is used, a hand rest or crutch for the right hand is essential in order to free the thumb for manipulating the four keys on the back of the boot joint. Many try to play the bassoon without this crutch, but a satisfactory technique is hindered by the fact that the thumb has to hold the instrument as well as work the keys. (See Illust. 3-B.)

A great many performers are now using the seat strap method of suspension. An old belt, preferably of the cotton webbing type, is fitted with a small hook. A hole is drilled in the rib on the bottom of the protective cap over the U joint on the side toward the player. A ring is then attached or the player hooks the strap hook directly into the hole. The strap is placed across the chair about midway between the front and the back of the chair, with the bassoon supported by the left hand and the side of the leg. A protective bar over the $B\flat$ and the $F\sharp$ keys is necessary to keep these keys from catching in the clothing. The crutch for the right hand is no longer necessary, but the thumb rest will have to be removed and turned around to form a rest for the first finger of the right hand. This rest should cover the lower post and rod of the $C\sharp$ trill key. (See Illust. 2-B.) The first finger will then come in contact with the thumb rest above the second knuckle. For a sitting position this method of suspension is superior to the neck strap. It takes the weight of the bassoon off the neck and also frees the right hand entirely from supporting the instrument. With a little experimenting, the weight on the left hand can be reduced to a minimum. The leg strap method is similar to the seat strap method, except that the strap is designed to encircle the leg.

The third method of suspending the bassoon is by means of a floor stand. This stand is similar to the saxophone stands used in dance bands, and it has the advantage of taking over the entire weight of the instrument. It is somewhat dangerous, as the instrument may inadvertently be knocked over.

The fourth method employs a spike attachment similar to that used for the bass clarinet. This spike is attached to the boot joint and is adjusted to different heights by means of two setscrews. The balancing of the instrument is left to the hands and the side of the right leg. The stand and the spike attachment are not generally recommended for use in schools.

PART II

The Reed

No matter how skilled a performer may become or how good his bassoon, he is constantly at the mercy of his reed. Although the beginner can use almost any reed (provided that it is easy to blow and produces a reasonably clear sound), the more advanced player will become increasingly aware of the importance of the reed in relation to his performance.

Even the finest reed is short-lived. So a player not only has to be able to find and adjust each reed to his own particular needs, but he must also have a constant supply of new ones from which to choose. The student who plans to play professionally should certainly learn to make his own reeds, but the majority of school bassoonists use what is commonly termed a "commercial" reed. Although all bassoon players should make at least a few reeds to help them better understand how to make their own adjustments, some do not have the desire or the time to construct many reeds. In any case, the bassoonist needs to know something of the reed situation: the different styles, sizes, and shapes which are made; how to select a playable reed; and how to adjust the reed to his own particular needs.

The bassoon reed consists of two main parts: (1) the body (or tube) and the lay; (2) the wrapping or the wires and binding. (See Illust. 6). The tube is that part of the reed which is rounded to fit the bocal and extends from the shoulder to the back end of the reed. Although this part must be perfectly round, the throat, which is the part of the tube from the second wire to the shoulder, may vary in shape from round to almost flat at the first wire. Some reed makers refer to the wires in reverse order; i.e., the wire under the binding is wire number one, etc. The lay is that part of the reed from the shoulder to the tip.

The beginner will not notice at first, or be interested in, the variety of shapes and sizes of bassoon reeds. As the student becomes acquainted with a variety of reeds from various sources, however, he will begin to notice that there are many differences. There are probably about as many different types of reeds as there are bassoon players. Some of these individual variations are due to inconsistencies in the reed maker's handicraft, but the major variations in shape, length, and style of lay which will be noticed are due to the different reed makers' backgrounds and concepts of how the bassoon should sound. This fact is often confusing to the young student and to the instrumental teacher who has not made a special study of the bassoon.

The student who has been fortunate enough to have studied with a professional bassoonist will not be concerned with different models of reeds since he will most likely use reeds made by his teacher. For the majority of school bassoonists who buy their reeds in music stores or from different reed makers, however, the difference in reeds is a very real problem.

Generally speaking, there are two basic types of reeds--the German and the French. The fundamental difference between these two types is in the cut of the lay. As the two reeds are held up to a light, it will be observed that the German reed has a dark area extending from the shoulder to about 1/8" from the tip:

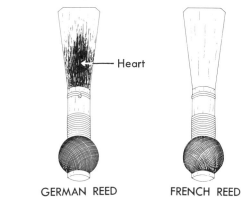

GERMAN REED   FRENCH REED

ILLUSTRATION 5
A comparison of German and French reeds

This area is thicker cane and is referred to as the "heart" of the reed (this heart can also be observed in some styles of clarinet and saxophone reeds). The French reed will not have any such heart, but rather will seem to be shaded evenly from the shoulder to the tip. It is the presence of this heart, or the lack of it, that causes the greatest difference in tone between the two types of reeds. It will be found that the French reed will have a light, "reedy" sound, almost nasal, while the German reed will be much darker and more mellow in quality.

There are many other small differences between the typical German and French reeds which can easily be identified; for instance, the blade of the French reed is usually wider and heavier throughout than the blade of the German reed. The throat appears to be wider and flatter in shape. The wires are heavier and trimmed off close to the reed instead of being twisted long and bent over as they are on the German reed. The binding is of heavier thread, and there

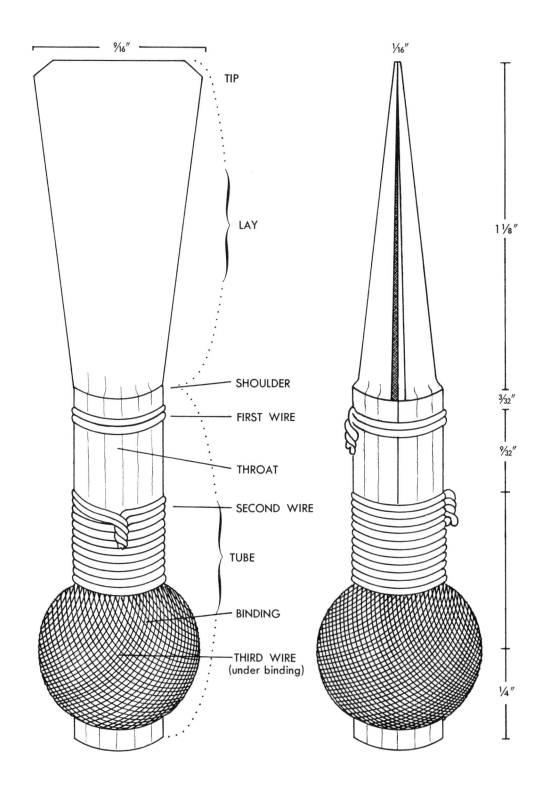

ILLUSTRATION 6

Parts of the bassoon reed, with standard measurements

is no attempt to make a fancy ball on the end of the tube. (In Illust. 9, compare the French reed [No. 2] with the others.) The usual color of the binding of the French reed is black, while the color of the binding on the German reed is usually red.

As was pointed out in Part I, the German or Heckel system bassoon has come to be the standard bassoon used in the symphonies and especially in American schools. Since the original French and German type reeds were made to be played on their respective instruments, it follows that the German type reed would be the standard reed. For the most part this is true, as the typical French type of reed is very seldom knowingly used on the German bassoon. While the Heckel system and the Conservatory system bassoons have remained true to their original design and form, the same cannot be said for the reeds. The two schools of reed making have been intermingled, in some cases to the extent that although the reed may look like a German reed, it may have the sound of the French reed. The part of the reed that makes the difference is the contour or profile of the lay. Often this is not easily discernible. While the light test will indicate something of the contour of the lay, the fingers and the thumb can also be used to feel what the eye observes. Not only should the longitudinal taper of the blades be observed, but, what is more important, the lateral proportions should be compared. The presence of the heart in the center of the lay will be felt with the fingers as a slight hump running down the center, tapering off to either side and toward the tip. The reed without this heart will feel smooth and even, although it will have the natural curve of the cane. This type of reed will be as thin in the center of the lay as it is at the sides.

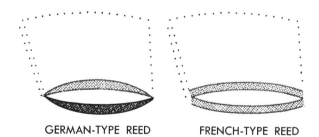

GERMAN-TYPE REED   FRENCH-TYPE REED

ILLUSTRATION 7
Lateral taper of the lay

This illustration shows the typical difference in lateral taper of the blades at about 1/4" from the shoulder in the German reed and the French reed. It is this thicker part of the lay that shows up in the light test as a darker area. Of course, there are infinite variations of this basic idea, all of which respond and sound differently.

There are at least three basic concepts of the longitudinal contour of the lay: (1) the parallel, (2) the wedge, and (3) the double-wedge.

ILLUSTRATION 8
Longitudinal contour of the lay

The parallel contour (1) is rarely made, as it is difficult both to make and to control. The wedge type (2) is quite common and is much easier to make. The French type reed is usually made with this contour in mind. The double-wedge contour (3) is probably the most popular because it has so many possible variants. The first wedge (3-A in Illust. 8) may vary from almost parallel to a decided taper, while the second wedge (3-B in Illust. 8) can vary from just the tip area of about 1/16" to as much as one half of the lay or more. Most well-constructed German type reeds are made with the double-wedge contour in mind, although the relative tapers of A and B will be different with each reed maker according to the kind of sound he wishes to produce and his concept of the proportions of the reed. Generally, the more heart there is in the reed the darker the sound will be.

Although the proportions of the lay itself are the most difficult to measure accurately, it is important that both the bassoon player who makes his own reeds and the one who buys ready-made reeds be well acquainted with this aspect of reed making in order that they may make or select reeds with more understanding of the relationship between the way the reed is made to the way it sounds.

A further examination of the commercial reeds being made today will reveal other differences of construction which are more easily distinguished and measured than those mentioned above. Although some of these differences can be attributed to errors and some to alterations due to the individual pieces of cane, most are modifications which have been made to suit the individual's bassoon and embouchure and not to those of the person buying the reed. Illust. 9 pictures ten commercial bassoon reeds from different sources.

Nine of the reeds pictured are made in the accepted German style and one (Number 2) is a typical French reed. Even a casual comparison of these reeds will show that there are several different concepts of the size and shape of the German bassoon reed. To further illustrate these differences, the reeds were measured and the results included in a chart which can be compared with the picture. (See Illust. 10.) These reeds were picked at random, and although they do indicate some of the most typical variations, no attempt has been made to illustrate all of the different ways bassoon reeds are made.

In general, the student will find two styles of reeds: (1) the short model, measuring from 2" to 2 1/16"; and (2) the long model, measuring from 2 1/8" to 2 3/8". The greatest majority of reeds will measure about 2 1/8", as the long model is the most common.

The short model reed will usually have a shorter lay (of about 1"), while the long model will have a longer lay of about 1 1/8". The width of the tip on almost all models is 9/16". While some will have a slightly wider tip, very few have one which is narrower. The size and shape of the throat on most models is about the same, because this is governed by the size of the opening of the bocal. The most common shape on the inside of the throat is elliptical, with a few being more rounded than others.

The spacing of the wires may vary considerably, as can be seen in the chart. This will often depend on the length of the tube. Although reed makers are not consistent in the distance used between the first wire and the shoulder, the distance between the second wire and the first wire is commonly little more than 1/4". Although iron, silver, and brass wire are used in the reeds in the chart, the most popular wire material is soft brass.

The most obvious difference in the reeds other than the length is the color and type of binding used, although this part of the reed is the least important. While cotton thread covered with red dope or lacquer is traditional, many other materials and colors are used, including black, orange, green, blue, and brown. The two most outstanding innovations are the use of a liquid plastic coating (Reed Number 8 in Illust. 9), and a plastic tube in place of the thread (not shown).

The differences listed above and shown in Illust. 7, 8, 9, and 10 are outlined so that the player may have a general idea of the way in which the bassoon reed, as it is made today, is modified to suit individual tastes. As might be expected, each of these reeds has slightly different playing characteristics and tone qualities; therefore, it will be necessary for the student to experiment with several different models before he can find which one will best suit his own particular embouchure and concept of bassoon sound. It should be pointed out, however, that not all the reeds, even those of one model, will perform equally well. This is caused by (1) the inconsistency of the reed maker's handicraft, and (2) the fact that each piece of cane is a little different. The bassoonist should not be too hasty in his decision about which model of reed is best for him. Clarinet

players, for instance, will often find only five, or even fewer, good playable reeds in a box of twenty-five. Although the bassoonist could expect a little higher ratio because of the difference in cost, he actually does little better in the long run.

The inconsistencies of making bassoon reeds by hand, especially the shaping of the lay, have always plagued bassoon players. It has long been felt that if the lay could be made by machine much of the labor and many mistakes could be eliminated. This has been the dream of many a bassoonist who has spent long tedious hours learning the art of turning out a playable reed. He has looked with longing at the clarinetist, who has only to add the final touches to his reeds. Although it will be several years before the bassoonist will be able to select a reed from a box of several precision-made reeds, there are now two sources of machine-made reeds.

Hugo Fox (Fox Products Corp., S. Whitley, Ind.) has successfully designed and constructed several different machines that cut the cane in proper lengths, gouge it, shape it, finish the lay, and wrap the finished reed. These machine-made reeds are superior to most commercial hand-made reeds in that purchasers are assured that the lay is cut the same each time and will have no thinned out places in the blades.

On the West Coast, Don Christlieb (3311 Scadlock Lane, Sherman Oaks, Cal. 91403) has also perfected precision machines which cut the cane, gouge it, shape it, and finish the lay. Although there have been machines available for several years that will cut, gouge and shape the reed, the two most difficult machine processes are the shaping of the lay and the assembling of the reed. Now that these problems have been successfully overcome, it should only be a matter of time before a cheaper and a more consistently made reed will be available to school bassoonists.

One perpetual source of trouble with reeds-- the cane itself--has given impetus to a search for a substitute material. Bassoon reeds are traditionally made from a variety of cane called Arunda Donax. For years most of the best cane used in this country has come from Southern France, but during shortages some cane has come from Spain, Mexico, and even more recently from sections of Southern California. The problem of a constant supply of usable cane plus the fact that the reed makers may get one quality one time and another quality another time have led to the search for a material that is easily obtainable and at the same time more consistent. The latest development in this line is a reed made entirely of plastic. The reed is molded in two separate parts and cemented together to form the finished reed. These plastic reeds have appeared on the market in recent years, and while they are certainly not as satisfactory as good cane reeds, it can be said that they are much better than many of

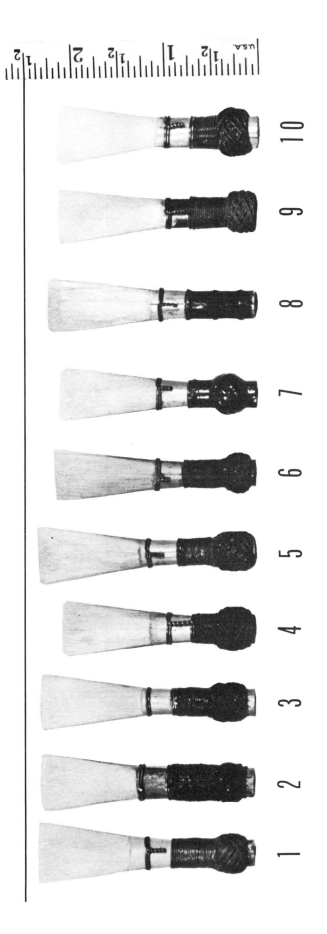

ILLUSTRATION 9

A comparison of ten commercial reeds

NUMBER OF REEDS	1	2	3	4	5	6	7	8	9	10
A. Total Length	2-11/32"	2-5/16"	2-5/16"	2-1/16"	2-3/8"	2-3/16"	2-1/8"	2-1/4"	2-1/8"	2-3/16"
B. Length of Lay	1"	1-1/16"	1-1/8"	1-5/16"	1-1/8"	1-1/16"	1"	1-1/8"	1-1/8"	1-1/16"
C. Length of Tube	1-11/32"	1-1/4"	1-3/16"	1-1/8"	1-1/4"	1-1/8"	1-1/8"	1-1/8"	1"	1-2/16"
D. Width of Tip	21/32"	20/32"	19/32"	19/32"	20/32"	9/16"	9/16"	17/32"	19/32"	8/16"
E. Width of Throat	10/32"	11/32"	1/4"	9/32"	1/4"	9/32"	9/32"	10/32"	10/32"	1/4"
F. Shape of Throat	E	F	E	E	R	E	E	E	E	E
G. Size of Wire	M	H	L	M	L	M	M	L	L	M
H. Type of Wire	B	I	S	B	I	B	B	B	B	B
I. Distance of First Wire from Shoulder	3/16"	0"	3/32"	3/16"	1/8"	0"	0"	3/32"	1/16"	1/16"
J. Distance of Second Wire from First	10/32"	10/32"	9/32"	1/4"	11/32"	10/32"	10/32"	10/32"	1/4"	9/32"
K. Type of Binding	Med Th	H Th	Nylon	M Th	Nylon	L Th	M Th	Pl	L Th	L Th
L. Color of Binding	Orange	Black	Red	Blue	Red	Red	Red	Brown	Red	Red
M. Thickness of Gouge	52	57	50	46	52	50	43	50	50	50

Note: All measurements are in inches except M which is given in thousandths of an inch.

F. Shape of Throat (E – Elliptical, F – Flat, R – Round)
G. Size of Wire (M – Medium, L – Light, H – Heavy)
H. Type of Wire (B – Brass, I – Iron, S – Silver)
K. Type of Binding (Th – Thread, Med – Medium, H – Heavy, L – Light, Pl – Plastic)

ILLUSTRATION 10

Comparative measurements of ten commercial reeds

the reeds that some students often attempt to use. If proper care is taken in their selection, the plastic reed will play surprisingly well (for beginners). Final adjustments of the lay can be made with a knife or file the same as with a cane reed.

One of the questions that invariably comes up when there is a discussion on bassoon reeds is the use of the single reed mouthpiece in place of the double reed. The idea is by no means a recent development, since it was first used around 1830 on an instrument called the Alto Fagotto. This was a small, bassoon-like instrument, and although the instrument itself was short-lived, the idea of using a single reed mouthpiece on a bassoon has remained. There has been some controversy among instrumentalists as to the quality of sound of this mouthpiece when compared to a double reed. The contention of some is that the listener cannot tell the difference. If there is no apparent difference in sound, one may as well use it, since the reeds are much less expensive and more easily obtained. The sound is quite pleasing if care is exercised in the selection of the mouthpiece and if the reeds are adjusted properly. Not all of these mouthpieces and reeds play equally well, any more than all clarinet mouthpieces and reeds play equally well. And it does not produce the same sound as a good double reed. For the performer, there is a great deal of difference in flexibility, in tonguing control, and particularly in ease of response in the upper register.

For the dance band musician, who must double on several instruments, this single reed mouthpiece might work quite well. In this case, a fine tone (such as one would need for symphonic or solo work) is not of prime importance, and the performer can use somewhat the same embouchure as that used for the clarinet and saxophone. However, the advanced bassoonist, who is interested in producing a true bassoon tone for solo and ensemble playing, will find this mouthpiece a poor substitute for a well adjusted double reed.

Selecting the Reed

The essential problems in selecting a reed are (1) to find out what factors make for a good reed and (2) how to detect those factors.

Probably the first question that the bassoonist asks about a reed is how it plays, the second is how it sounds, and the third is how it looks. The most revealing test of a reed is that of trying it on the instrument. Since in many cases it is impossible to try the reed on the instrument until after the reed is either purchased or finished (if the person is making his own reeds), it will be necessary to know those factors of appearance which will be an indication of the way the reed will perform and sound. The "hallmarks" of a good reed in terms of appearance are balance, symmetry of design, and

neatness in workmanship. These qualities are the result of superior craftsmanship in every phase of reed making. The experienced bassoonist learns to look for these factors in both the body of the reed (i.e., the lay, the throat, and the tube), and the wires and binding. The lay should be finished smoothly and evenly, with both blades balanced in taper. The edges will be even in thickness and will not overlap. The throat will be either elliptical or round, and the tube will be reamed smoothly and rounded expertly. The wires will be neat, snug to the body of the reed, and evenly twisted, but not so tight that they cut into the rind of the cane. The binding will be smooth and the windings evenly spaced. The detecting of these qualities is a matter of experience resulting from many comparisons of reeds by sight, feel, and playing. The following methods are offered for those who have had little experience with bassoon reeds.

1. The Lay. First, a check should be made to see that the lay is made in the accepted German style. This can best be accomplished by holding the reed up to a bright light. A lamp with a metal shade is best for this purpose. The reed should be held over the edge of the shade with just the blades showing in the light. If the lay is made properly, one should be able to see the shading as described in Illust. 11:

The lay should taper down in every direction toward the tip from this point.

a) The thickest part, tapering from the back toward the tip and to the sides.

b) A little thinner than (a) and tapering down into (c).

c) A little thinner than (b), gradually thinning out from (b) to the tip and from the center to the sides.

d) The thinnest part of the reed, which graduates out of (c) toward the corners of the tip. It will be noticed that the tip is slightly thicker in the center than at the corners.

ILLUSTRATION 11
The relative thickness of the lay

One blade of the reed should be compared with the other for balance of shading. The four corners at (d) should also be compared for even shading. Any exceptionally dark areas in (c) and (d) will indicate too much cane, while very light spots in (a) and (b) will indicate places where the cane has been gouged out too much. Reeds with thin places should be discarded, as they cannot be repaired, but dark areas, or the thick spots, can be scraped down.

The general contour and shape of the lay can also be checked by examining the outside of the blades with the fingers. Hold the reed so that light reflects off the surface at a slight angle. This will show up any imperfections, much the same as oncoming car lights will show up bumps and dips in the road. One will also be able to feel these imperfections with the finger tips. Of course, the lay should be sanded smooth and should be free of any cracks or splits which sometimes extend too far beyond the first wire into the lay.

A further indication of the shape and taper of the lay can be gained by examining and comparing the four edges of the blades and the edges of the tip. One may insert a thin, flat plaque so that the edges of the plaque protrude from the sides of the reed. The plaque will have to be inserted very carefully when the reed is dry. The four edges of the blades should be equal in thickness and taper at all points from the shoulder to the tip. Any unevenness in the edges will usually indicate a lack of balance in the lateral taper of the blades at that point. Checking the edges is particularly valuable in comparing the symmetry of the lay in areas (a), (b), and (c) as shown in Illust. 11.

Comparing the edges of the tip will show several aspects of the balance and contour of each blade and also the relationship of one blade to the other. The proper curve and balance of the blades of a well-made reed is diagrammed below:

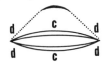

c) The center of each blade should be equal to the other in thickness and the taper to the corners should be the same on both blades.

d) The four corners should all be equal in thickness but thinner than the center at (c).

(Note: the letters (c) and (d) in this illustration correspond to the same letters in Illust. 11.)

ILLUSTRATION 12
End view of reed tip

While examining the tip, the distance across the tip and the distance between the blades in the center should be measured. The standard measurements are 9/16" across and 1/16" between the blades.

One should notice particularly to see whether the reed blades curve evenly and without wrinkles. The following diagram shows some typical deviations from the normal curve:

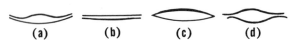

   (a)   (b)   (c)   (d)

ILLUSTRATION 13
Some typical deviations from the normal curvature of the tip

(a) Indicates that although the lower blade seems to be normal, the upper blade shows evidence of uneven scraping because of its waves. A slip of the knife at the tip can ruin an otherwise fine reed. The tip may be cut back and reworked if the gouged out places are not too thin.

(b) This profile indicates several possibilities: the tip area may be scraped too thin; the throat may be squeezed too flat at the first wire; it may not be a German style lay.

(c) This tip contour has many variations, but they are nearly all caused by the same error. If one will examine the first wire and the shape of the reed at the throat, he will probably see that the wire has been cinched too tightly and that the blade on the side of the "twisting" (in this case the upper blade) has more arch than the opposite side. This condition is usually accompanied by small splits which have continued from the forming of the tube into the back of the lay.

(d) The shifting of the blades indicated here usually takes place after the reed has been used. It is caused by the twisting action of forcing the reed on the bocal. It may also indicate that the cane has become very dry--a condition causing it to shrink away from the wires and binding. If the reed is superior in other respects and the shift is not so severe that it causes the reed to leak air, it may perform satisfactorily.

2. The Throat. Closely connected with the shape and contour of the lay is the shape of the throat. Many reed makers are not as careful as they might be in forming the reed at the first wire. Any unusual shapes at this point will often predetermine the shape of the lay, since the outside contour of the reed at the shoulders is one of the main check points for scraping-in the lay by hand.

The outside of the reed at the throat (directly under the first wire) should follow the natural curvature of the cane when it is gouged. If the first wire is twisted very tightly and is partly imbedded in the rind, it should be loosened about one-eighth of a turn. The second wire should also be loosened a little. One should look closely for cracks which may extend into the lay. A small crack in the center is not usually detrimental unless it extends more than a quarter of the length of the lay. Cracks on either side of the center, however, may cause the reed to be scraped in a lopsided manner.

If a student is making his own reeds, the symmetry of the two halves of the throat can be assured by using a temporary wire immediately back of the first wire, twisting it on the opposite side as a counter-balancing force. After the reed is formed and dry, this wire can be removed.

The inside of the throat will not always follow the outside shape of the cane exactly. The normal shape is anywhere from elliptical to almost round, depending on the reed maker's concept and methods. To inspect the throat, one should hold the reed up to the light and look in through the back of the tube.

The most typical shapes in forming the throat are:

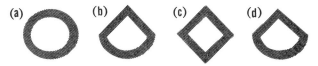

ILLUSTRATION 14
Four typical throat shapes

(a) This shape is normal and to be desired.

(b) The upper side has been squeezed to a point by twisting the wire too tightly and causing the reed to split in the center. This shape will cause the upper blade to have more arch; therefore, it will feel stronger, although it may be equal in thickness. (Compare with [c] in Illust. 13.)

(c) This shape is the result of squeezing too much with pliers on the sides of the reed when forming the throat at the first wire. Both upper and lower blades are cracked.

(d) This shape is the result of the same error as that in (b) except that the crack has formed to one side of the center.

The inside of the throat should be at least equal to the inside diameter of the small end of the bocal.

3. The Tube. The tube is that part of the reed which extends from the first wire to the back of the reed. Although the throat is usually elliptical, the tubing should be perfectly round, inside and out, from the second wire back.

CORRECT   INCOMPLETELY FORMED

ILLUSTRATION 15
A comparison of a correct and an incompletely formed tube

The most common fault is that of the tube being incompletely formed. This tube will leak along both sides when the bocal is inserted. If this condition is only slight, additional reaming may be all that is needed. If it is a great deal out of round, it will be necessary to use the pliers to remold the tube. One may check for small pieces of stringy cane which might have been left by the reamer. These can be removed with a small rat-tailed file.

4. The Wires. The wires are an important part of the bassoon reed. Not only do they hold the reed together after the tubing is formed, but their size, position on the reed, and tightness control to a great extent the manner in which the reed will perform and sound. The spacing on the reed will depend somewhat on the shape and style of the reed. Probably the most significant factor to be observed on a well-made reed is the neatness of wires and the way in which they have been twisted on. The two wires which are visible should be twisted on evenly and pulled up close to the body of the tube, so that they will come in contact with the cane at all points. They should not be cinched up so tightly that they cut into the rind

of the cane. This is particularly important for the first wire. Excess cinching will choke the reed and keep it from vibrating freely. One should not be too much concerned if the first wire is a little loose, especially if the reed was made several months earlier. When the reed is wet, the cane will expand and the wire will become tight again. Neatness and properly tensioned wires are one indication of a proficient reed maker.

5. The Binding. If the binding is made of cotton or nylon thread, as it often is, one should check to see whether the winding of the thread is evenly spaced on the ball. On reeds which have been in storage for several months, one should be careful to see if the binding is tight on the tube. Often the reed is made in a hurry and the binding is applied before the cane has dried sufficiently. As a consequence, after the binding is in place and the lacquer or dope applied, the cane continues to dry and shrink, leaving the third wire and the binding loose.

The color of the thread or the paint used will not in any way affect the playing of the reed. However, certain mixtures which contain a high content of plastic will be easier to mold if it is necessary to further shape the tube. Other materials are being used in place of the traditional thread winding. If they work as well as the traditional, there is no reason not to accept them. The two main factors to consider in examining the binding are its function and its appearance. One may ask two questions: (1) Does it hold the tube tightly in place without leaking and furnish a knob of some sort with which to handle the reed? (2) Is the binding neat and attractive, and does it show evidence of good workmanship? If the binding does not meet these requirements, it may be an indication that the reed is not well made in other, more important, aspects.

Finally, the quality of the cane itself should be considered. As no two reeds are exactly alike, only the more obvious aspects of color and grain can be observed. The outer surface of the bark or rind of the cane, as seen between the first and second wires, should be glossy or waxy in appearance. The color of well-cured cane will range from a light straw shade to a rich golden color. Brown spots which appear on the rind are not detrimental to the reed, but dark areas in the lay itself are to be avoided. Cane which has a greenish cast usually has not been cured sufficiently before the reed was formed.

Reeds with crooked or very coarse grain should be avoided. The grain can be seen as minute lines running the length of the reed. The spacing between these lines will vary from reed to reed, but it should be even. Uneven spacing will often indicate soft or hard parts of the cane. Close-grained cane will have more resistance and elasticity and will usually last longer than open-grained cane.

Although these methods of examining bassoon reeds are not by any means foolproof, the bassoonist can, with experience, be assured of a reasonably good playing reed if it shows evidence of balance, symmetry of design, and neatness of workmanship. Because of the unpredictable nature of the cane itself after it has been played a few times, it is almost impossible to be sure that one has a good reed merely by looking at it. Having selected those reeds which one thinks are good or which have possibilities, and having rejected those which are definitely impossible because of poor construction or inferior quality of cane, a person can proceed with the final testing methods. It is necessary to know what factors make for a good playing reed. Regardless of the style (long, short, French, German, or mixed) or who makes the reed, most bassoonists agree that a good reed is one that (1) is free-blowing, (2) produces a free, resonant tone throughout the range of the bassoon, (3) has good intonation, (4) responds quickly to a variety of articulation, and (5) is flexible and capable of dynamic contrast. In the detection of these qualities the bassoon player uses three methods: the sound and feel of the "crow", the "pop" test, and the actual testing and playing of the reed on the bassoon. Before testing the reed it will be necessary to make the following preparations:

1. Soak the reed.

2. Test the reed for air leaks.

3. Make sure that the bassoon is well regulated and without leaks.

First, one should soak the reed in water for approximately three to five minutes. He should insert the reed in water only up to the first wire, as soaking the entire reed may cause the tube to expand and the binding to become loose after the reed dries. Soaking the reed in water is superior to soaking in the mouth, as saliva is detrimental to the structure of the cane. A small bottle of water with a tight cap can be kept in the bassoon case just for this purpose.

Second, one should test the reed for air leaks along the seams of the tube and points where it fits onto the bocal. To test the reed for leaks, one holds the finger tightly over the end of the tube while blowing through the tip end as in playing. If the reed leaks at the seams, it may need more soaking to swell the cane or slightly more tightening of the wires. One should not cinch the wires too tightly, as such pressure may choke off the vibration of the blades. To test the reed for leaks on the bocal, one places the reed on firmly with a twisting motion, stops up the large end and vent hole with the fingers, and blows into the reed as he does in playing. If air leaks between the bocal and the tubing it may need further reaming or remolding with the pliers. One should ream very carefully, making sure the inside of the tubing is perfectly round. The bocal should fit into the end of the reed at least one-quarter of an inch. In some cases a small piece of fine sandpaper rolled on a match stick can serve to smooth out the inside. If the leak persists, it may be necessary to melt candle wax on a heated mandrel and apply it to the inside of the tube.

It is absolutely essential that these leaks be fixed before testing the reed. Even the smallest leak along the edge of the reed blades or between the reed and the bocal will give the impression of a very stuffy playing reed or instrument. It may be that the small end of the bocal is dented or damaged in some way. If this is the case, the bocal can sometimes be smoothed out with the end of the mandrel.

Finally, one should make sure that the instrument is in good playing condition. If there is any doubt, it is best that the instrument be checked with a reed already tested. This is important in the testing of new reeds. Many times a reed may be discarded or trimmed beyond repair because of testing on a poorly regulated bassoon.

After the reed is soaked, one should put it in the mouth and blow several preliminary "crows". (The process of crowing the reed is also called "buzzing". The sound that results is called the "crow", "cackle", "buzz", or "burr".) To produce the proper crow, the player places the reed lightly between the lips, using no lip pressure on the blades. The lips should be almost touching the first wire. Then start blowing through the reed and build up the pressure until the reed produces a double sound or crow. This crow should have both high and low pitched sounds present, with the low pitch predominating. Many bassoonists tune the pitch of the crow to third space E♭. The experienced bassoonist can tell a great deal about how a reed will play or how it needs to be adjusted by comparing the sound and pitch of the crow with the amount of breath pressure necessary to produce it. If the reed refuses to crow freely, it may need further soaking, or the tips of the reed may be too far apart. The standard measurement is one-sixteenth of an inch. After the reed is well soaked, one can squeeze the blades gently with the thumb and fingers to alter the opening. One should continue the crowing procedure until the reed produces a free-blowing, low-pitched double sound. In general, if the crow is high-pitched and hard to produce, the reed is either too far open, too stiff, or both. If the crow is too flabby in sound and too easily produced, the reed is either too close together at the tip, scraped too thin, or both. It is very seldom that one will find a new reed that is too thin. Most commercial reeds are usually left a little heavy to allow for individual adjustment.

The "pop" test is used to check for an air leak in the reed, as well as to check the stiffness of the blades. After having checked the reed for leaks along the seams, one continues holding the finger over the end of the reed and, instead of blowing, sucks all the air out of the reed and suddenly pulls the reed out of the mouth. The blades should remain closed for a second or two and then open up with a popping sound. The reed that will not remain closed at all is either too open, too stiff, or both. A reed that will remain closed more than two seconds is too much closed, too thin, or both. In order to learn just how long the blades should stay closed, it will be necessary to compare the results of this test with those of the crowing test and later with the way the reed responds on the instrument. In this, as in all aspects of reed making and adjusting, experience is the best teacher.

In testing the reed on the bassoon some like to check the reed for intonation first, while others prefer to test the tone and ease of response. Actually, it makes very little difference as to the order of the testing procedure, but it is a good idea to test each factor separately in order to focus the attention on that one factor alone. The following is a suggested procedure:

1. Ease of response and tone quality. Begin by playing notes in the middle register. Slow, slurred scales in the keys of F, G, and C are good. Gradually extend the scales down to the low register and then to the upper register. Listen carefully and compare the tone with the amount of resistance necessary to produce it.

2. Intonation. The accuracy of the reed can be quickly checked in the following manner:

a. Attack the third space E at a dynamic level of about forte. Compare this pitch with the E an octave below. Open and close the E key with the right thumb while playing the third space E. If there is a pitch change and the top E is flat, the reed is generally too soft. Next, begin a crescendo on this pitch and continue until the pitch "breaks down." If the pitch breaks too quickly with very little breath pressure, this is another indication of a soft reed.

b. Now play the E♭ on the third space with the forked fingering, i.e., first and third fingers. If this note is sharp in pitch, the reed is too stiff. Compare this pitch with the E♭ an octave below. A further check may be made by opening and closing the fourth finger (the B hole) and the B♭ key with the right thumb while fingering E♭ as above. If the reed is too stiff there will be a noticeable flatting of the pitch. If the reed is accurate, the quality may change slightly, but the pitch will remain true. Other notes which are useful for indicating a reed which is too stiff are the C♯ on the second space, D on the third line, G on the fourth space, and A on the fifth line. All of these notes have a tendency to go sharp with a reed that is too heavy or stiff.

Generally a reed that has a free, responsive, full tone and checks out accurately on the E and E♭ tests will perform well throughout the range of the instrument.

3. Attack. The reed should be tested next for attack in the low, middle, and high registers at various dynamic levels with a rapid staccato tonguing response. To test for attack, one may pick any note from the scale (C is good, as one can play the four C's from the very low to the high register) and try various attacks from pianissimo to fortissimo. A good reed should respond immediately in all registers. Any scale or staccato passage from a solo or from ensemble literature is good for testing the staccato response of the reed. The tip of the reed and the area just back of the tip are most responsible for a good attack and staccato. The width of the tip opening is also vital. It is at this point that the bassoonist usually needs to make most of the small adjustments necessary to fit the reed to his own embouchure and playing requirements.

In discussing the characteristics of a good bassoon reed, bassoonist Homer Pence, Assistant Professor of Music at Ball State University and a member of the Musical Arts Quintet, points out that patient, careful trimming and treating the reed will assure both staccato and legato articulations in all registers.[1]

4. Dynamic contrast and flexibility. A reed that is properly made and adjusted for a good tone, intonation, and attack will usually be capable of producing both a pianissimo and a fortissimo in all registers with comparative ease. Most reeds will need to be broken in over a period of three or four practice sessions, however, before they can be expected to respond with any degree of dependability. Although a reed may seem to do very well in a private practice session, it may not turn out so well in the ensemble or under actual playing conditions. Several reeds should be taken to the rehearsal and checked at that time. A knife and a plaque can be carried very easily and used during rests or breaks for any last minute adjustments. The flexibility of the reed is that quality which allows for wide interval skips with little effort. A reed that is not flexible may play quite well in either the low register or the very high register, but jumping back and forth will be difficult. Although for solo work it is imperative that the bassoonist have a reed that is equally balanced in all registers, it is fairly common practice for professional bassoonists to have reeds adjusted for special passages which appear in orchestral literature. A notable example is the famous bassoon solo in the first movement of Tschaikowsky's Symphony No. 6 in B Minor, measure 1. This passage is difficult to play softly on the bassoon unless a very soft reed is used. This procedure, however, should not be carried to the extreme, as the bassoon player can hardly hope to change reeds every time the music goes up or down. He should aim for a reed that is well-balanced in all registers.

It is almost impossible to select a reed, test it for playing characteristics and break it in without making at least a few minor adjustments. Nearly

[1]Homer Pence, "Characteristics of a Good Reed," Teacher's Guide to the Bassoon, (Elkhart, Indiana, H. & A. Selmer, Inc., 1963), p. 7.

all bassoon players learn very quickly the necessity of molding the curvature of the blades with the thumb and forefinger to either open or close the tip opening. Most students will have felt the need for even further adjustments and will have experimented with razor blades, knives, and sandpaper--often to the detriment of the reed. The teacher will need to know how to guide the student in his experiments with reed adjusting and, if necessary, arrange for the purchase of the essential tools.

Adjusting the Reed

If the bassoonist has been careful in his selection of the reed or in its construction (if he makes his own), the final adjustments should be only minor. Reeds are constantly wet while playing, and they generally react differently to the effects of saliva because of the differences in the density and composition of the cane. While some become softer each time they are played and need to have the tip cut back and the arch built up with squeezing on the first wire, others become stiffer and need to be scraped or sanded lightly over the entire blade. The reeds which seem to swell and become harder during the breaking-in period usually turn out to be the best playing reeds and last a longer time than others.

All single and double reed players have found that a reed will not do its best until the pores of the cane become smoothed and filled in. Some have even gone so far as to say the reed will play better after it is somewhat dirty. Single reed players hasten this process by laying the reed on a piece of plate glass and rubbing the surface of the lay with the finger. The bassoonist can do the same thing with the use of the shaped plaque. After the reed is wet, one should insert the plaque and rub the lay lengthwise with the finger tip. It is not advisable to use the flat plaque for this operation, as there is danger of splitting the reed. The smoothing or filling in of the pores can also be done with fine garnet paper, a fingerboard, or shave grass. After the reed has been played on and then allowed to dry, one may rub the entire lay with either of the above materials very lightly to remove the raised grain. If the grain continues to rise after each playing, a person should repeat this process each time until the reed becomes reliable. One should not use too much pressure, however, or he may remove too much cane and soften the reed.

The student who has not made bassoon reeds is often at a loss to know what to do to the reed if it needs adjusting and therefore will hesitate to do anything. Although the basic principles of reed adjustment are quite simple, their proper application requires much experience, which can be gained only by hours of experimentation and practice.

Stated very briefly, these basic operations are either to increase or decrease the resistance of the reed.

These operations are accomplished by either increasing or decreasing the arch at the back and the opening of the tip by squeezing the reed at the wires, or by increasing or decreasing the thickness of the reed blades at different points with the knife or file. Cutting off the tip of the reed in effect increases the thickness of the lay.

Illust. 16 indicates the adjustments that can be made by squeezing the reed at the wires with pliers and the areas on the lay to be scraped for various results. When squeezing or pinching the reed at the wires, care should be taken that one does not use too much pressure or the reed may crack. With practice, one will soon learn how much pressure can be applied safely. As a general rule, it is best to try an adjustment with the wires before scraping the lay thinner. This may not only save time, but it may also save the reed. Once it is scraped beyond a certain point it is almost impossible to restore it to playable condition. Most bassoonists, however, use a combination of squeezing at the wires and scraping when testing and adjusting reeds. The corrections most often necessary are for reeds (1) which are too stiff or hard to blow, (2) which have unevenly balanced blades, (3) which tongue poorly or attack sluggishly, and (4) which are too soft and flat in pitch.

1. The reed that is too stiff and hard to blow. Most reeds that are sold commercially are too stiff to play easily without some minor adjustments. This is due to both the seasoning effect mentioned earlier and the fact that most reed makers leave the reeds a little heavier in order to allow for individual adjustments. In either case, the reed merely has too much cane left in the lay. A reed that is hard to blow (too much resistance) may also have too much arch in the back and too wide a tip opening. In this case, one squeezes the first wire with the pliers from the top and bottom to decrease the arch at the back and reduce the width of the tip opening. If, after the tip opening is correct and the general contour of the blades looks even, the reed still blows hard, it will be necessary to reduce the thickness of the blades. One may then scrape or file the entire lay from back to tip. If the reed is too stiff, it will often be sharp in pitch, and the sound of the crow will be high-pitched and feel restricted. One should continue scraping and testing until the crow is free and low-pitched, and the reed no longer sounds sharp on the test notes. One should check frequently with the "light" and "feel" tests and be careful not to remove too much cane at any one time.

Usually a reed that is too stiff and sharp in pitch will refuse to speak immediately in the low register from F down to low B♭. The tone quality will also be rough and loud. In this case, file or scrape the back of the reed (area B in Illust. 16).

ADJUSTMENT OF BASSOON REED AT THE WIRES				
OPERATION	RESULTS			
	BACK	TIP	TONE QUALITY	PLAYING CHANGE
1. Squeeze 1st Wire from sides	More arch	More open	Darker, more robust Less reedy Higher pitch	More resistance Reed will feel stronger to lips Tonguing will improve in low register
2. Squeeze 1st Wire from top and bottom	Less arch	Less open	Lighter, more reedy Thinner Slight pitch drop	Less resistance Reed will feel weaker to lips Tonguing will improve in high register Reed will play easier in middle and high register
3. Squeeze 2nd Wire from sides	Remains about same	Less open	More reedy, but not as much as in No. 2	Less resistance Easier to tongue staccato Low register will not respond to fortissimo
4. Squeeze 2nd Wire from top and bottom	Remains about same	More open	Little darker Little higher pitch	Slight increase in resistance Low register will be stronger
5. Squeeze 2nd Wire from sides first, then 1st Wire from sides next	Much more arch	More open	Much darker and more robust Higher pitch	More resistance Reed will feel heavier and stronger to lips Light tonguing will be sluggish
6. Squeeze 2nd Wire from top and bottom then the same for the 1st Wire	Much less arch	More at first then less	Much thinner and lighter Reedy Pitch will drop	Much less resistance Reed will require very little lip pressure Up to a point, light staccato tonguing is easier
7. Squeeze 2nd Wire from sides then 1st Wire from top and bottom	Less arch	Much less open	Very reedy, thin and lighter than in No. 6	Even less resistance than in No. 6
8. Squeeze 2nd Wire from top and bottom then 1st Wire from sides	More arch	Much more open	Very dark sound More robust and heavy in quality Pitch is raised	Great increase in resistance Reed will feel much stronger to lips Improves fortissimo tonguing in low register

A GUIDE FOR SCRAPING THE LAY

A. (Area within dotted line) Scrape here to control the bass register. Should be left as thick as possible.

B. Scrape here to control bass register also and to bring out the low pitch in the "crow". Decreases resistance.

C. Scrape here to control an unstable B♭:

D. Scrape in this area to control attack and staccato tonguing. Scraping here decreases resistance. Cut tip back to increase resistance.

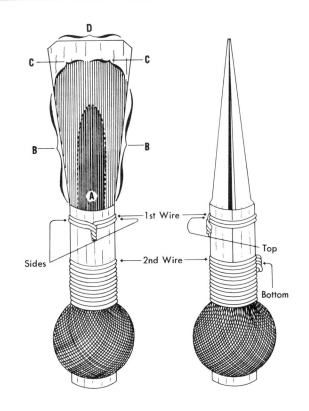

ILLUSTRATION 16

A chart of possible adjustments of bassoon reeds at the wires, and a guide for scraping the lay

If too much cane is removed from the lower half of the reed (areas C and D in Illust. 16), the notes from high G up to high E♭ may be affected.

2. <u>The reed with unevenly balanced blades.</u> In a good reed, not only should both blades be equally tapered and matched point for point to each other, but also each blade should be balanced with itself. A study and comparison of successful and unsuccessful reeds with the Dial-Indicator showed that in nearly all of the unsuccessful reeds there was a wide discrepancy in thickness between the two blades. The difference was often as much as ten-thousandths of an inch. The good reeds, on the other hand, showed agreement within one- or two-thousandths of an inch between each section of the two blades. There were also discrepancies found in the lateral balance of each blade, particularly in the areas just back of the tip. A difference of even one- or two-thousandths will make a difference in response, and a five-thousandths difference will cause the reed to play very poorly. On the other hand, small differences in the areas near the shoulder proved to be not too critical.

Although the Dial-Indicator is by far the most accurate means of determining the comparative measurements of the blades, the methods already described, when combined with the crowing and playing tests, can yield very good results. The light test described before will now be even more valid, as the soaked cane will let more light through. The shaded areas of each blade should be compared very carefully. The flat plaque can be inserted between the blades and by gently bending the plaque, first against one side and then against the other, one will be able to detect any difference in resistance. This bending test will also reveal any particularly thick or thin areas near the tip of one blade. When the blades are very wet, a person will notice the dark color of the plaque showing through at the corners of the tip. The more one can see the plaque showing through, the thinner the cane is at that spot.

For a more complete inspection of the back of the reed and the edges, one may insert the shaped plaque all the way past the point where the first wire encircles the reed. It will be necessary to pull the first wire down out of the way for this operation. Pressing the blades flat against the plaque will show up any humps or dips which may be present. Also, the edges of the reed will be more easily examined and compared for evenness of thickness and taper.

With a wet reed it is also possible to get an indication of the balance of the blades by gently pinching the reed blades from the top and bottom with the thumb and forefinger. By turning the reed several times and comparing the resistance of the two blades, one will be able to determine, along with the other tests, the relative thickness of the blades by their resistance. The thicker one will have less "give" than the thinner blade. This test will also indicate which blade has more arch. The blade with more arch will feel stronger even though it is the same thickness. Before deciding to scrape down the blade that feels stronger, it is advisable to examine the reed at the first wire. More than likely the first wire was twisted too tightly in forming the throat and has caused one blade to arch upward in a "V" (See Illust. 14 [b] or [d].) There will often be a small crack in the center of the reed running from the shoulder toward the tip. If the crack is not too decided, this problem can often be remedied by removing the wire and replacing it with another twisted on in the opposite direction. This will help re-form the shape of the throat, and unless the blades have been scraped unevenly, the balance can be restored.

A reed with one thick blade will have a crow that will feel and sound like a stiff reed. The reed will also feel very stuffy on the instrument and will be unstable in pitch.

Having found the area or an entire blade that is too thick or out of balance, one may use a knife for removing cane from small spots or a file if the entire blade is to be scraped. With hand-made reeds it is often necessary to remove excess cane from the middle of the reed. (Illust. 17.) This area is often neglected in the finishing of the reed because too much cane has been taken from the tip, where the observer can easily see and hear the results, and because of taking off cane from the back to free the low notes. If this is done without smoothing down the area between, there will be a "bump" or thick section:

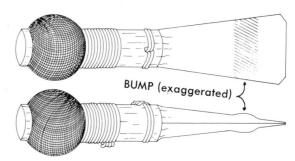

ILLUSTRATION 17

"Bump" caused by faulty scraping technique

It should be noted that this bump is due to the faulty scraping technique either on the part of the reed maker or on the part of the person finishing the reed. This pronounced bump is not to be confused with the slight ridge which appears on the double-wedge style of lay (Illust. 8). When finishing the double-wedge style of reed, this ridge should be controlled, of course, but not removed.

Irritating the inside of the reed blade tips with a fine emery board or garnet paper (use a slight rubbing action) will darken the tone and also provide an immediate, lighter, yet more overt, tone response. Bathing the bassoon reed in salt water will produce a like result. But permit the reed to mature for a few days before playing it.

In the final stages of finishing and adjusting a reed, many bassoonists have found that the B♭ just above the staff is "wild" (i.e., tends to play sharp or flat). This is often a balance problem, and by removing just the smallest amount of cane from the area just back of the tip and on the sides, the stability of this note will be improved (Area C, Illust. 16.) This area is very sensitive to the slightest change, so one should use only the finest reedpaper, pouncing paper, or shave grass for corrections.

3. The reed that tongues poorly. A reed may produce a low-pitched crow and play well in tune on the instrument and yet lack the capacity for rapid staccato and immediate attack. There are two factors which control the way the reed responds to tonguing-- the width of the tip opening and the thickness of the blades at the last 1/16" toward the tip.

If the reed will not produce an even and controlled attack in the low register from F to low B♭, the tip opening may be too narrow. One may squeeze the reed at the first wire to open the reed. This action will also increase the volume and make for a more robust tone in this register than would otherwise be obtained. If one does not wish to change the tone quality, he may squeeze the second wire from the top and bottom. This will open the tip but will not change the tone decidedly.

After adjusting the tip opening for attack and tonguing in the low register, it may be sluggish on staccato elsewhere. A person may work down the area just back of the tip very carefully with either the file or shave grass, depending on how much needs to be taken off. (See Area D in Illust. 16.) He should be careful that the center of the tip is slightly thicker than the corners. If the reed does not have the corners of the tip removed, he may cut a small triangle off each corner. This will often facilitate tonguing and will eliminate any objectionable "buzz" or "rattle" of the reed.

Care should be taken not to take too much off the tip, as this will make the high register notes difficult to attack. It may also make the reed play flat. One ought to work very slowly when adjusting the tip, and test the reed frequently. He may have a reed that responds well in the low and middle registers and still will not produce a good attack on high F to C. In this case, the tip opening may be too wide. Squeezing the first wire from the top and bottom will close the tip slightly. Also, one may squeeze the second wire from the sides. It will be seen that this is exactly opposite from the procedure used for adjusting the opening for attack in the low register; one will need to try for a happy medium in this respect.

4. The reed that is too thin or too flat in pitch.

It is very seldom that a person will find a reed that is flat to start with. It is only after making adjustments for a stiff or poorly balanced reed, or for one that tongues poorly, that the reed may become so thin and lacking in resistance that it plays flat. Reeds that have been played on for too long a period of time tend to get water-logged and seem to lose their elasticity. The remedy for this is to put the reed away for a time and let it dry out. If one is doing a great deal of playing, it is best to have two or three reeds to alternate. If the reed is in tune, but the entire bassoon is flat, the pitch may be raised slightly by reaming out the back of the reed so that the bocal may fit farther into the tubing. A shorter bocal may also be used.

A flat reed is usually one on which the tip area has been worked down too thin. The best testing spot is the E on the third space. (This testing procedure has been described earlier.) Another indication of a too soft reed is that the high B or C will not respond quickly to a direct attack. The tone quality of this reed will usually be thin and reedy. The sound of the "crow" will be almost all low-pitched with very little if any high-pitched sounds present.

If the reed is otherwise satisfactory and the tendency to go flat is only slight, it will often improve with continued use. If it does not improve, then one may clip off a hair-line (about 1/64") of the tip with the knife. Lay the tip on the cutting block and cut with a rocking motion from one side to the other. Another very useful device for trimming reeds is a pair of end-cutting nippers, which can be purchased in a hardware store. After one has cut a very little off the tip, he may not have to do any more. If the reed still plays flat, clip off another 1/64". If as much as 1/16" must be cut from the tip, it will usually be necessary to rework the entire lay, as the balance will probably have been destroyed.

The pitch can also be raised by squeezing the second wire from the sides and then squeezing the first wire from the sides. If this makes the reed too sharp (check the forked E♭), scrape the reed from the shoulder forward in Area B, Illust. 16. This will lower the pitch again and also darken the crow.

It can be seen that it is impossible to adjust and test the reed for just one factor alone. One must test frequently for flatness if he is working on a reed that is sharp. If one is working on the tip of the reed to improve the staccato, he should constantly check for flatness and upper register attack. Always work for a happy medium.

Additional Suggestions

The following additional suggestions may help when adjusting reeds:

1. Have the reed well soaked with water before playing and especially when trimming or scraping.

Soaking for two to five minutes should be sufficient--oversoaking will cause the cane to become brittle.

2. Do not hasten the breaking-in process, but spread it out over several playing periods in order to allow the cane to season between times. It is best to have several reeds in different stages of development, rather than waiting until one reed gives out or breaks before starting a new one.

The best reed is no longer the best performing reed. Such a reed has reached its maturity peak and therefore has to be on the downgrade. Look for another reed which might have a better response at concert time.

3. Remove very little cane at a time unless you are very sure of what is being done. Cane that is once removed cannot be replaced. Crow the reed and test it on the instrument between each adjustment.

4. Always play-test reeds before any performance or rehearsal. Since most recitals and concerts take place during the evening hours, the temperature drop during these hours will adversely affect the response of the reeds. A sudden rainfall or an extreme change in temperature, either up or down, will affect the cane—and with the cane, the reed response. Plan to make the final, last-minute adjustments at the rehearsal under performance conditions. A reed that sounds fine in the studio often will not sound at all well in the group or on a solo.

Change reeds during a performance only if absolutely necessary.

5. Do not spend too much time adjusting a reed at one sitting. After a prolonged session, one will find that he would not know a good-sounding reed if he heard one. Short scraping sessions and frequent comparisons with a reed which plays well is desirable in order to keep the ear tuned to the sound for which the performer is working.

6. No two reeds are exactly alike. Every now and then one will find a reed that refuses to respond to any treatment. Put it away and try it again at another time. If this does not help, do not waste time on it. Throw it away.

7. Although many small, last-minute adjustments can be made by squeezing or pinching the reed with the pliers at the first or second wire, the performer will find some reeds that will only respond to squeezing at the first wire. This is due to the way the reed is constructed. If one makes his own reeds, it is possible to make the adjustment of the reed with the wires more effective by the following method:

With a sharp knife or file, begin a beveling operation after the cane is shaped and before it is folded:

ILLUSTRATION 18

Bevels to assist adjusting of reed by squeezing at the wires

Begin the bevel at the point (a) where the first wire will encircle the reed. The pitch of the bevel should be increased to its greatest angle at the second wire (b), then decreased until it is out by the third wire (c). The depth of this bevel should be the greatest at the second wire, where it coincides with the thickness of the cane. Four such bevels will provide a natural fulcrum at the first wire and will help in the adjustment of the tip opening by squeezing the second wire. These bevels should be cut very carefully. Too great a bevel will negate its purpose. A bevel which slices into the rind will narrow or distort the tube. The greatest value of the bevels will be to help the second wire to control the opening of the tip. It will be noticed that the arch of the blades at the back of the lay is affected very little by the second wire. Each individual will have to experiment with his own reeds in order to learn just how much pressure to apply and which combinations of squeezing either the first or second wire will work best.

Tools for Adjusting Reeds

The tools necessary for finishing and adjusting of bassoon reeds are pictured in Illust. 19. It is suggested that if the school owns bassoons these tools be purchased by the school and kept with the other tools and equipment for the care and repair of instruments. The student who owns his own instrument should have his own set of tools. It is best to buy these tools from a supplier of double reed equipment, but if a person is creative or knows someone who can do it for him, several of the essential tools can be made.

1. The Plaque. Although the plaque is the smallest and the least expensive piece of equipment, it it quite indispensable. There are two models--flat and shaped (1a and 1b in Illust. 19). The flat models are made from spring steel. A satisfactory flat plaque can be made from six-thousandths spring steel, which can be purchased at a large hardware store. The shaped model is made in the form of an arrowhead, being tapered in such a way as to fit the curvature of the inside of the reed.

2. The Reamer. The reamer should be purchased from a supplier of bassoon reed equipment. There are several models on the market, with varying numbers of cutting edges. Some have as many as

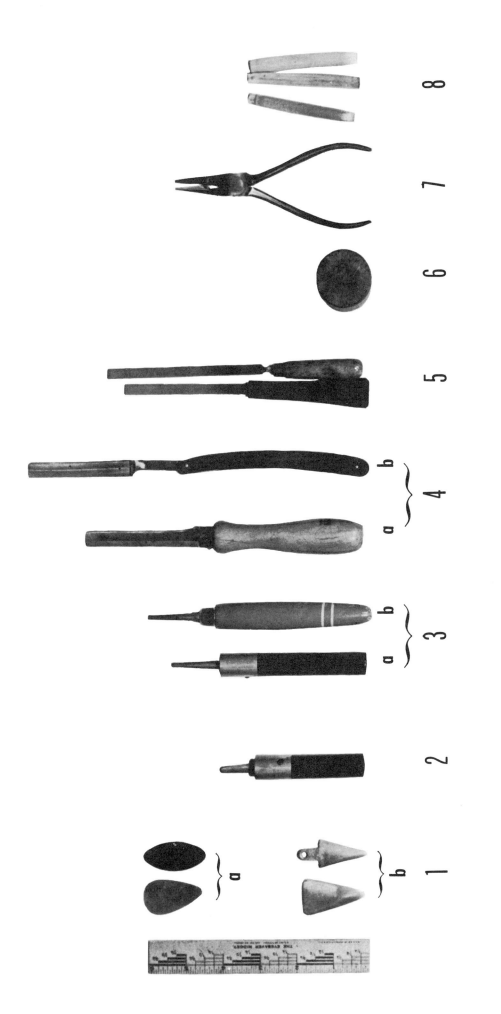

ILLUSTRATION 19

Tools for adjusting bassoon reeds

1) Plaques   3) Mandrels   5) Files   7) Pliers

2) Reamer   4) Knives   6) Cutting Block   8) Dutch Rush

five or six cutting edges, but the best and most efficient reamers have only one or two. The taper of the reamer should be the same as the end of the bocal. If there is any question of which reamer matches the bocal in question, it would be best to try several before buying one.

3. The Knife. The scraping knife should be made of the finest steel and be capable of holding a very sharp edge. Knives made especially for reed scraping are by far the best to use. They can be purchased either in a straight or a folding model. A good grade pocket knife with one blade that has a perfectly straight cutting edge can be used at first, but one will eventually need to get a good reed knife for the best results. Many bassoonists have had excellent reed knives made from old straight razors by grinding down the thin edge to a blade no wider than 1/2". (4b in Illust.19.) The original sides can be left on for carrying in the case, or these can be removed and a wooden handle attached for bench work.

Along with the knife, one will have to have a sharpening board or stone. The type of stone which has one coarse side and one fine side is best. Stones can be purchased either from the hardware store or from the reed tool supplier.

When using the knife, one should always scrape the reed from the shoulder toward the tip. Scraping in the opposite direction will raise the ends of the reed fibers because of the bevel. Tip the back of the blade forward toward the tip of the reed, so that you will scrape instead of cut. If the cutting edge of the knife is tipped forward it may enter the fibers too deeply and create a weak spot that will ruin the reed.

4. Files. Some prefer to use files instead of knives to finish reeds. Others like to use a combination, since there are uses both for the file and the knife. If the performer has not been in the habit of using a knife, perhaps the filing technique would be safer for him to begin with. Nickolson Piller files, Numbers 0, 1, and 2 are best for fine work (the larger the number the finer the file). These files can be bought in 4", 5", or 6" lengths. Some bassoonists use the Nickolson three-cornered files in the same sizes. One can buy these files either from a reed tool supplier or in large hardware stores. Cleaning equipment for the file can be either a small wire brush or an old toothbrush.

5. The Mandrel. Although a precision-made mandrel is absolutely essential for the making of reeds, it is possible to use a substitute if one is only finishing reeds. At this stage, the mandrel is used mainly for holding the reed while scraping or filing the lay.

A substitute mandrel can be made from a screwdriver, a small punch, a pancake turner, or some other kitchen utensil. The metal stock of the mandrel should measure 1/4" in diameter. The stock should be cut off with a hacksaw to 1 1/2" from the handle. Using a grindstone or emery wheel, one should taper the stock down to 1/8" at the end. The length of the taper should be no longer than 1". It should then be polished with emery cloth. (No. 3b in Illust. 19 is made in this manner.) The best mandrels are made from brass stock. There are two lengths of mandrels for purchase--long for forming the reed and short for holding the reed while finishing it.

6. Cutting Block. The cutting block is also called a "Billot". This is a small, round piece of very hard wood or plastic with a flat or slightly convex top which is used when cutting the tip off a reed. It can be purchased only from a reed tool supplier.

7. Pliers. A small pair of narrow-nosed, side-cutting pliers can be purchased either in the hardware store or from a reed tool supplier. For the person who is interested only in adjusting the completed reed, almost any of the small pliers on the market will be satisfactory. The pliers are used in adjusting the wires and for making small changes in the shape of the tube and the throat of the reed.

8. Abrasives. Several abrasive materials are used in the final stages of reed finishing for polishing the blades, closing the pores, or for taking off just the smallest amount of cane. These materials are Dutch rush, garnet paper, pouncing paper, and emery boards.

Dutch rush is also known as Horsetail, and is popularly called either "file grass" or "shave grass" by various reed men. It is a tubular shaped grass that grows in jointed sections. It is green in color and is found in moist, shaded places. The outside of the grass is grooved like a file. It can be used either wet or dry, and is useful for taking off a minute layer of cane in one spot or over the entire reed. When it is used dry, it serves as a polisher to help close the pores of the cane.

The preferred grade of garnet paper is 8/0, and it can be purchased in hardware stores. Special reed paper, which can be used wet or dry, is available also from reed tool suppliers. Pouncing paper is a very fine grade abrasive which is usually found only in paint stores. The emery boards can be purchased in dime stores. These are also known as finger-boards, and are used for filing the fingernails. One side of the board has coarse garnet paper, and the other side has fine paper.

9. The Dial-Indicator. The Dial-Indicator is a precision gauge with which the bassoonist can measure any part of the lay or throat of the reed within one-thousandth (.001") of an inch. Up to the present time, any improvements in the making of reeds and in the selection of ready-made reeds have been the result of trial and error. Although this gauge is by no means a substitute for the trained eye and hand, its use can take much of the guesswork out of measuring and adjusting the lay. The workman can still make faulty judgments, but errors which are caused by lack of balance and symmetry can be avoided.

ILLUSTRATION 20

The Dial-Indicator

    A) Dial Indicator   C) Pointer Arm

    B) Contact point   D) Adjustable stand

To measure the thickness of the blade, one slips the pointer arm between the blades of a reed, allowing the contact point to ride on the top side of the blade. The contact point moves up or down according to the thickness of the reed blade between it and the end of the pointer arm. The thickness is read on the dial, which is marked off in thousandths of an inch.

A series of marks which indicate the distance of that mark from the tip are etched on the top of the pointer arm:

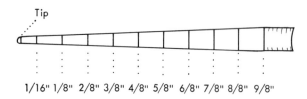

ILLUSTRATION 21

Detail of pointer arm

These marks will aid in comparing the same spot at the same distance from the tip on both blades. As a starter, one might make a comparison between a successful reed (one that has proven itself in performance) and the reeds which have failed for one reason or another. As an aid to charting the contour or shape of the lay in thousandths of an inch, a sample chart is included (Illust. 22.)

Although good reeds can often be purchased in a music store or from a music jobber, the most satisfactory reeds are usually obtained from the reed makers themselves.

Care of the Reed

The bassoonist, having once found a good reed, will usually guard it with his life; nevertheless, he may unknowingly be cutting down the effectiveness and the life of the reed by faulty habits of care.

The reed should be kept clean on both the outside and the inside. The overabundance of dirt and scum which seem to accumulate on the reed can easily be scraped off with the fingernail each time the reed is played. A light sanding with very fine reed-paper about once a week will help to keep the reed looking clean and will also take care of the gradual stiffening of the cane. If the reed is very dirty, it can be scrubbed with a mild solution of soap and water and an old toothbrush without harm if the reed is rinsed well afterward. Girls who wear lipstick should be particularly careful that the lipstick is not allowed to cake on the reed.

The inside of the reed should be kept as clean as the outside. The best method of cleaning the inside is to swab it with a small feather. If the feather is wider than the edges of the reed, one can trim it down with a pair of scissors. To clean the reed, insert the tip in a small glass of water; then run the feather in through the back of the reed until it comes out at the tip. Pump the feather up and down until all the food accumulation has been removed. Never insert the feather through the tip end first. A pipe cleaner may be substituted for a feather. If the reed is exceptionally dirty, a mild solution of soap and water may be used. The reed may then be rinsed with clear water as before, but do not use hot water. If food and saliva are allowed to dry inside the reed they will actually hinder the vibration of the blades. Even running clear water through the reed occasionally will help. The performer may blow the excess water out of the reed by blowing through the reed from the tube end. He should wipe the blades dry before putting the reed away. Some players use a solution of peroxide to clean out and restore very old reeds. This will not harm the reed and will sometimes revive an otherwise useless reed for a short time.

The proper storage of the reeds is important. A good reed case is essential. The reed should not be kept in the glass or plastic vial in which some commercial reeds are sold. After the reed has been used, it should be allowed to air and dry. The plastic tube is air-tight and will cause the reed to mildew and deteriorate very rapidly. A reed case that is air-tight will be just as bad. Reed cases can be purchased in a variety of sizes and styles. By far the best type is one in which each reed is held on a small mandrel. Such placement keeps the tube from shrinking or getting out of shape between playing sessions. The most practical size is that which holds three reeds. In an emergency, a small box lined with cotton will do quite well. The average life of a good reed is only about three to four weeks if it is being used every day. With the proper care, cleaning, and storage, one can expect reeds to last several weeks longer than they otherwise would.

Innovations in Reed Making with the "Reeduall"

A new process developed by the Rabco Company under the direction of Saul Roberts consists of taking half of an old but well-performing bassoon reed and mounting it, the "model reed upon the jig,"[1] in order to copy and create a match for it. As a key is duplicated by a locksmith, an old bassoon reed may be matched in size and dimensions to precise and exact measurements. The steps of wiring, wrapping, and forming the reed take only six minutes. In a matter of minutes a performing bassoon reed can be constructed and produced from a shaped (dry) piece of cane.

[1]Saul Roberts, President, Rabco Reeds, P.O. Box 782, North Miami, Florida.

Reed No. _____   Date _____ 19 ___

| SIDE A | | | | SIDE B | | |
Left	Center	Right		Left	Center	Right
46	47	46	9/8	44	46	45
39	40	35	8/8	36	40	38
36	39	32	7/8	33	38	36
33	37	30	6/8	33	37	35
30	34	29	5/8	30	35	31
27	31	28	4/8	26	31	28
24	27	25	3/8	24	27	26
20	23	22	2/8	18	22	20
12	17	13	1/8	10	14	13
10	13	11	1/16	8	12	10
6	11	8	Tip	7	10	8

REMARKS:

ILLUSTRATION 22

Sample chart for recording contour of the lay

The figures in the center column correspond to the marks on the pointer arm. Side A is for one blade, and Side B is for the opposite blade. It is recommended that the side on which the first wire is twisted be called Side A to avoid confusion later. The numbers in each square are the readings taken from the Dial-Indicator at that spot. The table has been filled in with readings from a good reed as an example of how to use the table. The diagram of the best reed should be kept for reference and comparison with future reeds. It is not recommended, however, that the gauge be used at every step of cutting the lay or in adjusting the reed. It should be used only to check now and then to see whether one has strayed too far away from the original measurements. On the other hand, the inexperienced player will find it very useful at first to measure all doubtful reeds in order to help him make a more satisfactory selection. It can also be used in teaching reed making, to show students their mistakes. The Dial-Indicator can be purchased from Christlieb Products, 3311 Scadlock Lane, Sherman Oaks, Cal. 91403.

PART III

Tone Production

Within the limits of a good instrument and reed, the main factors of producing a beautiful, singing tone on the bassoon are (1) a clear concept of the bassoon tone, (2) correct habits of breathing and breath control, (3) a correct embouchure, and (4) an appropriate vibrato.

The student's concept of the tone and his ability to understand and apply these basic factors are, to a great extent, dependent on his inborn musical capacity, general intelligence, emotional and physical make-up, and his capacity for applying himself. Even the exceptionally talented student, nevertheless, may often develop faulty habits of breathing, embouchure, or vibrato. These faulty habits can sometimes be attributed to an inferior instrument or reed, but for the most part they are caused by the lack of good musical training and a general misconception of how the bassoon should sound and how it should be played.

The first and most important step in producing or teaching any kind of tone is for the person concerned to have in his mind's ear a clear concept of the tone he wants to reproduce. If a professional bassoonist is available, he should be used for demonstrations as often as possible. Otherwise, radio, television or disc and tape recordings should be used. The recordings are the best, of course, since they can be played over and over for a critical study. With the increasing popularity and availability of high fidelity records and record playing equipment, this kind of listening can be even more valid than it was several years ago. Although records of the major symphony orchestras can be used to good advantage in the study of the bassoon tone, the solo and ensemble records are much better. The number of these recordings has increased a great deal in the past few years. Until recently, most of the available solo bassoon recordings have been made in France. Even though the performance is excellent for the study of tempo, phrasing, articulation, and other phases of musical interpretation, the tone is that of the French bassoon. Since there is considerable difference in the tone quality of the French and the German bassoons, recordings made by bassoonists using the German sound should be used for the study of tone. The recordings made by Pezzi, Schoenbach, and Christlieb are to be particularly recommended. (See p. 72 for a listing of solo and ensemble recordings.)

As the teacher gains more listening experience, he should begin to form a mental image or picture of the desirable characteristics of bassoon tone. Not only must he be able to hear and feel these things himself, but he must also be able to convey what he hears and feels to the student. Not every one will agree in every instance to the following description, since each person has his own way of describing what he hears, but the important thing is a satisfactory end result.

Probably the first characteristic of a good tone is that it sounds and feels to the listener as if it were produced with perfect freedom and without apparent effort. The tone color may be described as being dark, mellow, or round. To some it may be pictured as hollow and "woody" like the sharp staccatos of the marimba or xylophone, but with a definite edge of "reediness". The buzz of the reed should be evident, but not so reedy as to sound like the saxophone. The low and middle registers should be rich, full, and robust, while the tones of the high register have been described as sounding ethereal, haunting, and rather like the human voice in that same range. Finally, it will be observed that a vibrato which is similar to that of the voice has become a part of the modern bassoon sound.

Further study and comparison of the tone quality of various bassoonists will reveal small differences even within the basic German sound. As was seen in Part II, the style of the reed itself may vary considerably, according to the individuality of the performer and his concept of how the bassoon should sound. As an example, one may listen to the recordings of Leonard Sharrow, who gets a little different sound from that produced by most bassoonists by using a very thinly cut reed (similar to the parallel construction in Illust. 8) on a Heckel system bassoon. Many would like to imitate his tone, which is very pleasing, but the reed is difficult to make and control. The teacher and the student may have to listen to several different performers before they decide which particular sound they like best and which they would like to imitate.

Actually, in the hands of a competent performer, the bassoon is capable of a wide variety of color and style within a basic tone. This will depend on the mood and character of the music, the style of articulation, and the register of the bassoon used. To many, the bassoon is thought of only as the 'Clown of the orchestra". Although it is true that the bassoon can depict humorous and ridiculous moods better than any other instrument, it is unfortunate that this nickname has stuck with the bassoon. This is only one small part of its capabilities.

Bessaraboff emphasizes the versatility of the bassoon by saying:

The bassoon has a peculiar ability to express the most contradictory moods, varying from the solemn to the ridiculous, from the gay and happy to the pathetic and lugubrious. Only the bassoon can so well express droll and clownish moods or become impertinent, even impudent. To call the bassoon "the clown of the orchestra" is to insult this noble instrument.[1]

Composers have long recognized the versatility of the bassoon tone, as its various uses in modern orchestral works indicate. No other instrument can depict so well the ethereal, mystic, and haunting melody in the opening measures of Stravinsky's The Rite of Spring, or the plaintive song in the "Berceuse" of his Firebird Suite. While these examples are in the high register, Tchaikowsky chose the middle register for the solemn statement of the first theme in the first movement of his Symphony No. 5 and the low register for the melancholy and despair of the first movement of Symphony No. 6. Yet another example of the versatility of the bassoon is the role of the gruff Grandfather in Prokofieff's Peter and the Wolf, using the blustering, reedy, and rough qualities of which the bassoon is capable in the extreme low register. The sharp, brittle staccato sound which is used, for example, in the theme of the brooms in Dukas' Sorcerer's Apprentice is well known by anyone who has listened closely to the background music for humorous situations and grotesque actions in Walt Disney cartoons. Additional examples of the use of the bassoon's wide variety of style and color can be found in almost any of the orchestral music available today. These particular examples are cited since they can usually be found in any record collection.

For the teacher, then, who is not primarily a bassoonist, it is possible to make use of selected recordings for a study of tone and for awakening the aural imagination of the student. Developing a concept of tone requires more than merely passive listening. It also requires that the student experience this tone in his own playing, both physically and aurally. Since the early training of the student has such a vital bearing on his ability to hear and feel what a good tone is, inferior instruments, poor reeds, and misconceptions of breath control and embouchure may make it necessary that he re-learn not only how the tone should sound but how it should feel.

The importance of teaching the student the physical sensations of a good tone as well as to hear it is brought out by Mursell in speaking of the teaching of a good vocal tone:

We should make the child tone-conscious through proper motor placement... The rightness of the feel of his singing, and of its sound, are two aspects of exactly the same thing. They both work together, and one checks up and sustains the other.[2]

Waln, in an article on the development of playing maturity, also emphasizes the importance of connecting the feel of a good tone with a recognition of the sound of a good tone.[3]

The student will need to experiment with tone quality and, with the help of the teacher, change his embouchure, breath support, size of mouth cavity (by thinking various vowels), adjusting the reed, etc., until the right combination for a freely produced tone is found. If the student is not already aware of the feeling of the tone as well as the sound, the teacher can call his attention to this by merely asking him how the tone felt to his breath and embouchure. If the student does not know, the teacher can ask him to play it again as he thinks how it feels. Gradually, by trial and error, the student will learn to feel as well as hear the "rightness" of his tone.

At the same time, tonal studies to extend the feeling and sound of a good tone throughout the entire instrument should be practiced. One such study is to select a tone on the bassoon which is beautiful and freely produced and which comes the nearest to the sound that is being imitated. B♭ on the second line is usually a good tone with which to begin. Hold this tone and then slur down chromatically to the next tone below. Make the second tone as much like the first as possible. Then play the first tone again, and go down the chromatic scale two tones in the same manner. Practice in this fashion from the selected tone to the bottom of the instrument and then from the selected tone to the top of the range.

The bassoonist should continue to check frequently with the recording of the bassoon tone he is attempting to imitate. Recording the student's playing so that he may hear his tone as others hear it will also be very instructive. Often a tone that sounds good to the performer sounds dull and lacking in resonance to the listener.

One of the best methods of developing tone consciousness is through concentration on playing in tune. Many students think that they are playing in tune if they put the keys down and blow, but it is doubtful if they are really aware of the results. Even the best of bassoons will not play in tune automatically. In both solo and ensemble playing, the performer will need to make small adjustments in embouchure and breath support constantly in order to play with good intonation. At least a part of every lesson should

[1]Nicholas Bessaraboff, Ancient European Musical Instruments (Cambridge, Massachusetts: Harvard University Press, 1941), p. 125.

[2]James L. Mursell and Mabelle Glenn, The Psychology of School Music Teaching (New York: Silver Burdett Company, 1938), p. 273.

[3]George Waln, "Playing Maturity Requires Training and Careful Listening," Instrumentalist, 11:30, October, 1956.

be devoted to getting the student to hear and feel the pitch of the tone <u>before</u> he plays it on the bassoon.

Singing is by far the best experience in developing pitch discrimination, since the performer must be able to hear the pitch or melody inwardly before he can sing it. If the student is playing a particular note out of tune or phrasing poorly, the teacher should ask him to hum or sing the passage. After doing this, the intonation or phrasing will improve because the student is playing what he hears. If the student can learn to "sing" on his instrument, his tone quality, intonation and general musicianship will all improve.

Other experiences which are excellent for developing pitch and tone discrimination are (1) playing familiar folk tunes and melodies by ear, (2) matching tones played by the teacher (the student should not be able to see which note is being played), and (3) playing all scales and chord patterns without music.

Any improvement in the student's tone quality on the bassoon, however, will depend to a great extent upon his ability to control the tone. The high school or college bassoonist will usually have a rather clear concept of the kind of sound he wants to produce, but improper breath control and embouchure (gained as a result either of poor instruction in the beginning or faulty habits which have been picked up later) make it impossible to realize this sound.

Having discovered for himself the way the bassoon should sound and the capabilities of the instrument, the teacher will be in a much better position to listen critically to the student's playing and to diagnose his problems. The use of recordings for the study of tone does not relieve the teacher of the responsibility of learning to play the bassoon to the best of his ability. This accomplishment should also include the adjusting and modifying of reeds, since this is so closely related to the problems of the embouchure and breath control. Actual experience in the problems of playing the bassoon does several things for the teacher, even though he may not be able to play it well or does not intend to continue beyond a certain point.

First, he will be able to demonstrate as well as to talk about the various factors of tone production; for example, he will be able to demonstrate the correct bassoon embouchure as well as to describe it. This ability will not only save much time but will certainly be more meaningful to the student. Everyone recognizes the value of an actual demonstration as opposed to a mere explanation.

Second, even though he may not actually demonstrate the procedure, the teacher will be able to speak with conviction. He will know that this method of breathing or that style of embouchure works because he has tried it himself.

Finally, the teacher will be able to feel within himself what the student is doing right or wrong, as a result of having experienced the same problems.

Breath Control

Good breath control, or breath management, is recognized as one of the most important physical skills necessary in playing any wind instrument. Breath control involves correct breathing habits, an open and relaxed throat, balance with the embouchure, and resistance of the reed.

There should be no problem with correct breathing habits for playing the bassoon, as this breathing is the same as that used for such natural functions as talking, coughing, sneezing, or simply getting enough air for breathing. These correct breathing habits can readily be viewed in the rise and fall of the abdominal muscles of the baby or young child, or even a cat or dog. All people are born with these correct habits, but somewhere along the line they are replaced by bad breathing habits, which, if used when playing an instrument or in singing, produce poor results in tone and support.

A great number of students get the idea that they must do something special when asked to take a deep breath. Some of these mistaken ideas include the raising of the chest and shoulders, sucking in the stomach muscles, stretching the neck, and tucking the chin down against the neck. It should be pointed out to the student that none of these excess actions are necessary; in fact, they are actually detrimental to good breathing. Nearly every case of incorrect or shallow breathing seems to come from a misunderstanding of the part of the body or muscles used in good breathing plus a slumping posture which makes it almost impossible to expand the lower section of the chest area.

The two sets of muscles used in correct breathing are the muscles of the lower ribs (the intercostals) and the diaphragm. Although one cannot feel or see the diaphragm itself as it works up and down, he can both see and feel the result of its working in the expanding and contracting of the hollow between the ribs from the breast bone down to the belt line. When one takes a deep breath, this area will bulge. As the air is let out, this area will sink in or contract. The action of the lower rib muscles can be felt by placing the thumb and fingers of both hands just below the last rib, with the thumbs in the back and the fingers in front. In the taking of a breath, the action of these muscles will force the thumb and fingers apart. In correct inhalation the feeling is a general expansion down and out in all directions. The usual mistake is to try to breathe using only the upper chest and shoulder muscles. In these cases the student is rarely aware of the proper muscles or muscular action involved in good breathing habits.

Good posture is the first requisite for making proper use of the diaphragm and lower rib muscles in breathing. Good posture is primarily a matter of body balance and controlled relaxation. The head should be held high, but with the chin extended neither up nor down. The body should be held erect, but not stiff. The chest should be held high, with the shoulders back and relaxed. When one is standing, the weight of the body should be balanced on the balls of both feet, and the feeling should be one of readiness to move out in any direction. A good test of body balance when one is in a sitting position is to ask the student to stand quickly. If he has to shift too far forward in order to rise, his posture is not balanced. The arms are held in a natural way, neither tightly against the body nor extended out in a strained position. It will be found that this alert, ready-to-go position of the body, whether sitting or standing, will help the mental attitude of the player as well as make good breathing possible. It is next to impossible to have the body in an alert, eager attitude without the mind being alert also. On the other hand, a slouched position of the body or standing on one leg or sitting with the legs crossed can only indicate that the person is not mentally alert.

One of the objectives of a balanced posture is to free those muscles used in correct breathing and to relax all other muscles. Playing with a relaxed feeling, notwithstanding, does not mean that there is no effort or work involved. There is a great deal of work involved, but this work should be directed to the diaphragm and lower rib muscles and not to the upper chest and shoulder. Excess tension in the area of the shoulders and neck will not only be wasted effort but will also interfere with the proper action of the correct breathing muscles.

The problem for the teacher of the bassoon is to instruct the pupil properly. There is no one set procedure, as each student presents a little different problem. A perfectly good method for some might not work at all for others. Since the teacher cannot force the student to breathe correctly, he can only hope to lead him to realize the possibilities of natural breathing. This can best be done by demonstration and through indirect suggestion.

The following methods have been used by many teachers in getting the student to feel the action of the diaphragm and rib muscles: (1) the blowing up of balloons, (2) coughing while placing the thumb and fingers around the waist just below the lower ribs, (3) shouting "hey" or any similar explosive sound with real emphasis, (4) laughter of the body-shaking type, (5) panting like a dog while holding the hand over the stomach, (6) cinching up the belt very tightly to emphasis the expansion in that area, and (7) lifting a heavy object while holding the breath at the same time.

The important factor at this point is to make the student aware of the correct muscles involved and their control. Once this is accomplished, it will be only a matter of continued practice until this control becomes automatic. To gain control of these muscles after they have been located and felt, the student

would do well to practice breathing by itself before attempting to apply this new experience to playing the instrument. A very good exercise is to breathe in and out rapidly to get the feeling of expansion and contraction. Next do it slowly, in and out. Finally, take the breath in as fast as possible but let it out very slowly, making sure that the breathing muscles and not the muscles of the throat are holding the breath back.

The student and the teacher should not expect to get results overnight, since the old habits may have been developed and used for several years. It will be necessary for the teacher to continue to watch carefully for indications of old habits creeping back, especially when the attention is directed to other phases of playing.

Quite often, students who have been using the wrong breathing muscles tend to be in too much of a rush to start the attack. They often begin blowing even before the embouchure or fingers are in place for a particular note. Without any preparation whatsoever, they will begin. This indicates that the student is unprepared both physically and mentally. After the student has gained sufficient control of the correct breathing muscles, the following procedure may be helpful in correcting this habit of beginning before he is ready: (1) have the body and the instrument balanced and in a comfortable position; (2) have the first note in mind (or better yet, the entire phrase), the fingers on the holes or keys, and the embouchure set and ready; and (3) finally take the breath quickly and begin the tone without any hesitation. This routine should be practiced very slowly at first, with the teacher observing and listening closely. The teacher should be on the alert for any signs of undue tension, particularly in the throat muscles. Students who have had the habit of taking a breath before pitch, fingers, and embouchure are ready usually stop the air with the glottis. If this habit is allowed to continue, it will show up in guttural sounds and grunts as the student plays. These sounds are a sure sign of a closed or constricted throat. In following the correct starting procedure (provided that the reed is responsive) the tone should become fuller and more resonant. After the student is able to attain a full, rich sound without tension and with the proper use of the breathing muscles, he is then ready to practice by himself.

Although correct breathing habits are only one factor in the whole problem of breath control, the teacher should expect the following results from the proper use of the diaphragm and lower rib muscles after a reasonable length of time: (1) the tone should become bigger, more resonant, and more freely produced; (2) intonation should be improved; (3) longer phrases and more expressive playing with a properly produced vibrato will be possible; and (4) a full breath can be taken in an instant. None of this can be fully realized, however, unless the student is able to understand completely and apply the concept of the open and relaxed throat. This concept is closely related to the use of the correct breathing procedures in good breath management. The student may very well be using the correct breathing muscles but he will be unable to attain full support of the tone throughout the range of the instrument because of a constricted throat. The teacher will find this to be particularly true with the student who has tried to develop a vibrato too early. Usually the student will not realize the controls necessary to relax the throat. To tell him to relax will only serve to make him tighten up all the more. The teacher should be on the alert for signs of tightness or constriction in the throat muscles, since the student is usually quite unaware of this problem until it is pointed out to him.

The indications of a constricted throat are often found to be (1) grunting or guttural sounds made while playing, (2) a fast, uncontrolled tremolo, (3) a strident, harsh tone quality connected with a tendency to play sharp in both the very low and high registers. These effects are caused by excess tension in the neck and throat and the closing, or partial closing, of the glottis. The closing of the glottis is natural in the act of swallowing, coughing, cutting off the air when swimming under water, or holding the breath to lift a heavy object; however, the muscles that tighten the throat and close the glottis must be completely relaxed for the free production of tone.

Because these muscles are usually controlled by reflex rather than by direct thought, the teacher must resort to indirect methods of suggestion. The following have been found to be successful: (1) ask the student to yawn and concentrate on how the throat feels; (2) take a full, quick breath through the open mouth and exhale with the throat feeling the same as it does when inhaling; (3) have the student exhale warm air on the hand as is often done when steaming eyeglasses for cleaning; (4) concentrate on imagining that the head is a complete vacuum while playing long tones; and (5) imagine that one is projecting the tone right through the instrument and out to a point or area across the room. Any one or several of these suggestions will usually emphasize the idea of the open throat to the student. If the habit of a constricted throat has been well established, it will be necessary to direct conscious effort in playing with more relaxation in this area for a long time before it will become automatic.

It will often be found that the student who has been playing with a closed or constricted throat is using a reed that is too stiff. This student will be using the muscles of the neck and the embouchure to overcome the excess resistance of the reed instead of using the larger and stronger breathing muscles. Before the feeling for a relaxed throat and correct breathing can be realized, the reed will have to be adjusted to vibrate more freely. The proper functioning of the embouchure will also have to be taught at the same time.

The Embouchure

Many problems with the bassoon embouchure at the advanced level are really breath control problems. It is well to remind the student in this respect that the bassoon is a wind instrument, not a lip instrument. Many try to force the bassoon to respond by biting and pinching the reed instead of using breath pressure forced through the end of the reed. In most cases where the student is using the jaw to bite or pinch the reed, he will also be using a constricted throat and very little push from the diaphragm or lower rib muscles. Again it will be found that the student has formed these habits by using a reed that is either too stiff or too wide open at the tip. In getting this reed to vibrate, he will set his breath pressure at about medium and then begin squeezing and biting the reed together until it produces a sound. The solving of this problem will be a matter of gradually finding the proper balance of breath pressure, reed resistance, and embouchure pressure. These accomplishments will take time and experimentation, but progress will be made only as all three phases are brought into proper focus and balanced with each other.

The functions of the lip muscles are to connect the wind column with the reed and to control the vibrations of the reed. Neither of these functions requires an excess use of the jaw muscles as seen in many faulty embouchures.

The two most prevalent problems with the bassoon embouchure are too little reed in the mouth and the biting action mentioned above. If the reed is to do its best work, the lips must allow it to vibrate-- not make it vibrate. In order to find the best spot on the reed for the maximum vibration, the student should experiment with the reed only. He may start blowing the reed with just the tip between the lips and gradually put more into the mouth until the lips touch the first wire. At some point along the lay, generally with about half or three-quarters in the mouth, he will find that the reed will produce the maximum of buzz, or "crow". It will be noticed that at the tip only one sound or pitch is heard, but as the buzz point is reached, a double-pitched sound will be produced. This will be true, of course, only if the reed is properly made and adjusted.

The most popular concept of the bassoon embouchure, and the one which will produce the best sound, is that which straddles this buzz point with the upper lip more forward (or closer to the first wire) than the lower lip. This is known as the over-bite idea. Some call it the "Andy Gump" type of embouchure.

The formation of this embouchure can be accomplished very easily by the combination of three factors: First, accentuate the natural overbite of the upper teeth over the lower teeth. Second, make sure that the angle of the bocal from the instrument to the mouth is downward rather than either straight or at an upward angle. Most bocals are made to angle downward, but occasionally one will be found that has been bent up. (Illust. 23-B shows this downward angle of the bocal in relation to the bassoon and to the player. Notice the overbite.)

The third factor is to adjust the position of the bassoon so that, with the head and body in a normal playing position with the player looking straight ahead, the reed will strike the cleft between the lower lip and the chin as it is brought toward the face. Then, by slightly inclining the head (Illust. 23-A) a person should have a comfortable and correct angle. It will be seen that when all three factors are used together, the lips will be placed in a straddled position around the buzz point of the reed without any undue contortion.

Both the upper and lower lips must be folded over the teeth so that very little of the red part of the lip is showing. The upper lip will almost touch the first wire when in proper position.

The action of the lip muscles should be one of folding or bunching around the reed rather than being pulled back smoothly, as in a smile. The smile action is found most often with students who have been transferred from another instrument such as the clarinet. The proper action has sometimes been described as being like the drawstring neck of a marble bag. Or, the student can be instructed to form the lips as in whistling, with the lips sucked in instead of puckered out. Using the finger in place of the reed can also be instructive. The teacher can ask the student to grip his finger with the lips only (no jaw pressure), making sure to exert equal pressure on all sides of the finger. In this demonstration, one has the added advantage of being able to feel with the finger, as well as with the lips, the action of the lip muscles.

If the student has been in the habit of not putting enough reed in the mouth, the use of the above embouchure will produce a noticeably darker amd more mellow sound--an accomplishment which is, of course, desirable.

The problem of the lower jaw, the chin muscles and the cheek muscles is universal in teaching all of the reed instruments. In all cases, the jaw muscles are used sparingly, if at all. The placing of two pieces of wood or cork about one-half inch thick between the back teeth while playing will demonstrate how little the jaw muscles need to be used. This is a good method to use with students who have the habit of biting the reed. The use of these blocks of wood will produce a noticeable freedom and an increase in the volume of sound, as it will be necessary to use considerably more breath pressure to operate the reed.

Along with the biting of the reed and the excess use of the jaw muscles will usually be the puckered chin. The teacher will be able to see that the chin is bunched up toward the reed and the skin appears to be full of indentations or dimples. There will also often be an air pocket between the lower lip and the teeth. The student will usually complain of a sore lip where the lower teeth cut into the inner part of the lip. Another indication of this habit is the reed that is bent upward on the bocal from the pressure of the jaw and chin muscles. The tone will be thin and pinched in sound and there will be a tendency to play sharp and with poor control in the high register.

As with all of the woodwinds, the chin muscles must be stretched <u>downward</u> so that the chin is pointed and the skin is smooth and tight. The following methods can be used for getting the student to feel this new concept: (1) for boys, have the chin pointed or pulled down as in shaving; (2) for girls, imagine that they are applying lipstick to the lower lip; (3) place the lower lip between the teeth, and, biting down lightly, pull the lip out with the chin muscles; (4) hold or smooth down the muscles of the chin with a pencil while the student is playing. If the chin muscles collapse while playing, after the student has learned their correct use, the teacher may call attention to this fact by merely touching the chin with a pencil or the finger tip.

The cheeks should be smooth, but should not be stretched tightly or sucked in. Some have trouble with the cheeks puffing slightly, especially if they are concentrating on a relaxed and free jaw action. If the student does not have control of the cheek muscles, the teacher may ask him to squint his eyes to help gain the necessary control.

The use of a mirror is indispensable in the correction and teaching of the embouchure. Since the student usually cannot <u>feel</u> what is wrong, it is most helpful if he can <u>see</u> it. The mirror should be used during practice periods until the student can feel the correct embouchure without having to observe it. It is a good idea to check in the mirror periodically for any slips or changes which might unknowingly occur.

The teacher should be able to demonstrate wrong embouchures as well as the correct one. Not only will this help him better to understand the problems of the student, but he will also be able to teach by imitation.

It will be noticed that the above procedures have little to do with the actual blowing of the instrument. They are only a means of getting the student to feel the proper sensation of the muscular action. It is suggested that some time be spent with the reed alone before trying these embouchure concepts with the instrument. Usually the student will do fine until he puts the reed in his mouth and blows. Quite

ILLUSTRATION 23

Side view of correct playing position and bassoon embouchure

often, at this point, his embouchure will collapse. The reason for this is usually more than just an embouchure problem; it is also a breath control problem. If the student is using the correct breathing muscles, it will only be necessary to instruct him to use more air pressure to compensate for the lack of jaw muscle pressure which he has been accustomed to using. After the student can produce a good solid sound with the reed only, he should try the same thing with the complete instrument. It will be necessary to have him practice only the easiest of material during this stage, since the breaking of old habits will require a great deal of concentration.

Little has been written in regard to the movement of the reed on the lips or the changes in embouchure pressure when changing from register to register. This is very seldom mentioned by the teacher, since any mention of it will usually cause the student to exaggerate this movement. However, instruction is often given the student in regard to the change of breath pressure as he ascends or descends the scale. The tension of the embouchure is usually taken care of automatically. The difficulty is that one will quite often tend to over-do this embouchure change and consequently cause the upper register to be sharp and pinched in sound. This is especially true if good breath control is not being used.

These two processes -- the changing of breath pressure and the movement of the reed in and out -- when properly balanced can help considerably to obtain a full, resonant, and tuneful sound from the lowest to the highest note.

Many have experienced difficulty in playing in tune the notes from F below the bass clef down to low B♭:

Ex. 3

Usually these notes are sharp. This may be caused by too much breath pressure, too closed a throat or too much reed in the mouth. Taking a little less reed in the mouth is the first and easiest condition to correct. At the same time, the player should part the teeth more than previously. The next step will be to get that open, yawning feeling in the throat with just the slightest letting up of the breath pressure. These notes will be better in tune and easier to tongue more rapidly with this relaxation of the embouchure, throat, and breath. When attacking any of these notes, the jaw can be lowered at the moment of attack, but it should be brought back up to the normal position immediately.

Many students have difficulty with the intonation and quality of the notes from F above the staff up to high E♭:

Ex. 4

Naturally, the breath pressure should be increased as one ascends the scale, but the usual tendency is to also increase the bite, or jaw pressure, in playing these high notes. Some even try to play these notes with the lip and jaw pressure only, which is entirely incorrect. In either case, the result will be a very sharp and thin, pinched sound. The jaw should by all means remain open or dropped down. The reed, however, may be moved slightly farther into the mouth as one ascends the scale. This movement is not as noticeable going up the scale slowly as it is in a wide interval leap of an octave or more. It is important not to allow the reed to slip on the lip; rather, let the lip move with the reed. This movement is accomplished by moving the instrument in or out with the left hand.

As an illustration of the action of the reed in connection with the lip, one may place the finger tip on the back of the hand and move the finger back and forth without allowing the finger tip to slip on the surface. Then let the skin move with the finger. It will be noticed that the skin becomes first tight and then loose, according to the movement of the finger. This is the same action that one will secure with the reed and the lips. This small tightening of the surface of the lips, plus a slight moving in toward the first wire, will allow the student to play these high notes with greater ease and with better intonation than he formerly had (provided that he is furnishing enough breath pressure to produce the pitch). For a direct attack on the high C, D, or E♭, it will usually be necessary for the upper lip to almost touch the first wire and actually to grip the reed with more force than usual. However, this is an unusual case. Even then, after the tone begins, the embouchure pressure should be slacked off to normal for that register.

The student bassoonist and the teacher should be careful to remember that any change in embouchure should be very slight. If one observes a fine performer demonstrating these changes, he will notice very little difference. Any exaggeration, especially in regard to changes in the upper range of the bassoon, will negate the results. As the player matures, these embouchure and breath changes become so automatic that one often does not realize they are being made. This is somewhat like shaping the mouth in talking. One generally does not have to give any conscious thought to what goes on physically when he says a given word or letter unless he is learning a new language or something is wrong with his diction.

Then, in the effort to make the correction or learn the new sounds, he is very conscious of what he does with his mouth, tongue, teeth, and lips. Before he can make use of the new language or the corrected diction, it must be practiced until it becomes automatic before there can be any fluency. The same principle applies, not only to the embouchure changes, but to the correction of problems dealing with all phases of tone production.

The Vibrato

The fourth factor in producing a beautiful, singing tone on the bassoon is the development of an appropriate vibrato. In spite of the fact that there are still some teachers who insist that vibrato cannot be taught or refuse to discuss it at all, questions from advancing bassoon students must be dealt with. The student hears the vibrato every day on the radio, in the concert hall, and on recordings, and often tries to imitate it. Students are eager to know what it is and how they can produce it. The teacher who is confronted with these questions cannot side-step the issue, but must go in search of ways and means to teach the vibrato.

The vibrato as used in artistic bassoon playing is very close to that used by good singers. Vibrato is a periodic pulsation or fluctuation of the pitch, intensity, and timbre of the tone. Studies of the vibrato of artistic voices indicate that the rate of the pulsations may vary from five to eight pulses per second, but that the average seems to be between six and seven pulsations per second.

The vibrato is produced by an oscillation or quivering of the muscles used in the production of tone. In the case of the bassoon, these include the diaphragm, the lower rib muscles, the muscles of the throat, and the embouchure. Although some bassoonists report that they produce their vibrato with the throat or with the lips and jaw, by far the most desirable and artistic vibratos are produced by involving the larger muscles used in correct breathing. A study made by Chapman of the solo chair woodwind player of fourteen major American symphony orchestras indicated that the greatest number of bassoonists favored the natural and the diaphragm vibrato over the use of the throat and lips.[4]

While some teachers feel that there is a difference between the natural and the diaphragm vibrato, it is the opinion of the writer that these are actually produced in much the same manner, except in cases where the natural vibrato involves the wrong muscles. The natural vibrato seems to be learned by unconscious imitation when the conditions are right. The person using it does not usually realize he has a vibrato as such until someone tells him about it. The diaphragm vibrato, on the other hand, is usually induced by a conscious effort to set the breathing muscles in a pendulum-like action or oscillation in order to produce the desired fluctuation. With practice, this action can become automatic, and after a period of time it will also feel natural.

One must first master the basic elements of breath control, embouchure control, and all the other techniques of playing. Some students will be able to develop the vibrato along with these other elements of playing musically, while others may never be able to develop a really artistic vibrato sound. The teacher will need to be careful to keep the vibrato problem in its proper relationship to the entire matter of producing a good sound, and should not allow it to become an end in itself. The student should analyze as little as possible; rather, his attention should be focused on the total musical effect (except when a specific defect or a faulty technique is detected).

The vibrato is not a cure-all for faulty intonation, or for a tone which is lacking in quality because of improper production. It can only embellish a good basic sound. One well-known bassoonist makes this point clear by comparing the vibrato with the whipped cream on strawberry shortcake: "If the cake is no good the whipped cream won't help it much!"[5]

Many students, however, seem to hear the vibrato to the exclusion of the sound it enhances, and consequently think this is the answer to all of their tone problems. Both the teacher and the student must realize that an adequate control of the vibrato, like many other factors in the production of a beautiful sound, cannot be learned in a short time. It is acquired in stages after a long-term study accompanied by gradual changes in musical concept and maturity.

Not every student who learns the vibrato by himself does it wrong. In fact, most talented students who are told to "make the sound sing" can find the necessary muscular action without any special instruction. Still, the teacher must be absolutely sure that the student is using the correct breathing muscles with good control and is playing with an open and relaxed throat. Usually difficulty arises when the student attempts a vibrato at too early a stage of development and without any aid or guidance, and uses the wrong muscles.

The most common vibrato mistake is that which involves the throat muscles. This is especially true if the student is playing with a tight, constricted throat normally. At first, this vibrato may seem to work out quite well, and the resulting sound will be quite acceptable; but as time goes on, the throat action often becomes quite uncontrollable. The vibrato becomes much too rapid and irregular in form and the basic sound thin and pinched. Because of the bleating sound, this is often popularly called

[4]Norman C. Chapman, "The Manner and Practices of Producing Vibrato in the Woodwind Instruments" (unpublished Doctoral thesis, Teachers College, Columbia University, New York City, 1953).

[5]Remark made by Sol Schoenbach, first bassoonist of the Philadelphia Symphony, at a woodwind clinic in 1954.

the "nanny-goat" vibrato. One will also begin to hear grunts and other guttural sounds in connection with the tone production.

It can be seen that this is not so much a problem of vibrato concept as it is a problem of poorly developed or wrongly developed physical skills. To correct this type of vibrato, the teacher will have to insist that the student play with a perfectly relaxed and straight tone until such time as the basic factors of breath control, embouchure, and resistance of the reed and instrument can be brought into proper balance.

The teacher will no doubt meet much resistance from the student at this point, as the player is seldom aware of the kind of sound he is getting. A simple demonstration of his vibrato as compared to the more desirable type can be given, using a tape recording of his sound. This can easily be compared with a recording of a professional bassoonist. A visual demonstration can be prepared also, by using the Stroboconn. The pitch fluctuations can then be seen as well as heard. Of course, the most ideal situation is for the teacher to be able to demonstrate both the right and the wrong ways.

It is not generally recommended that a teacher who is not himself a competent bassoonist initiate vibrato training. If the student is not sufficiently aware of the existence of the vibrato to be interested in learning to use it, he is not ready for it to be mentioned. On the other hand, the student who is ready for and interested in producing the vibrato but who is not able to find the correct muscular adjustment can sometimes be assisted in getting the oscillation started in various ways.

Suggestions such as were mentioned in finding the proper breathing muscles may work: i.e., saying "hey" with force several times in succession, laughing, or panting. One device that seems to work quite well is to have the student whistle "Yankee Doodle" to start the action, then reduce the whistling to a whisper, but keep the same rhythm going. Resistance to the breath can be set up by blowing through a very

small opening in the lips. It must be remembered that these are only suggestions to get the action started if the student cannot find it himself. Once the student has the basic idea, development of vibrato should not be a major problem.

Since it is essential that the vibrato be regular and perfectly even in all registers, problems of irregularity can sometimes be solved by practicing the vibrato in definite rhythmic groupings of two, three, and four pulsations per beat. A metronome can be used to set the tempo. One may start the metronome at about 100 and gradually increase to 120 beats per minute. He should then practice on a single note. After the feeling is established, move on to scales. The teacher should watch carefully to see that the action does not slip up to the throat, but is kept in the large breathing muscles.

It is essential for one to keep in mind that any such practices as described above are for the express purpose of finding and regulating the vibrato action. They have nothing to do with the artistic use of the vibrato in musical expression. After having isolated the problem of the vibrato for analysis and study, it must be returned once again to its proper place in the total musical picture.

The artistic use of vibrato in the bassoon tone is not something that the performer decides to put in here or there for a special effect. Vibrato control, like the other physical skills of tone production, must become so automatic and so much a part of the bassoonist's playing habits that he is not required to give any conscious thought to its use. He will then be able to turn his attention to the more important matter of discovering the expression demanded by the nature of the music he is performing. The teacher should constantly be on the alert to hear if the student is really expressing the musical content of a composition. The techniques of tone production should never get in the way of musical meaning.

Again, the student should study the recordings of recognized artists for a concept of how the vibrato is correctly used.

PART IV

Articulation

The term "articulation" is used here to designate the general manner in which the tongue, the breath and the fingers are used--separately or in combination--to group a series of notes into rhythmic patterns. The problems of articulation will be discussed under two headings, tonguing and fingering, with the idea of helping the student develop these skills to the point needed for the performance of the more advanced literature encountered in solo and ensemble playing.

Tonguing

Many of the student bassoonist's articulation problems are due to an incorrect use of the tongue. In order to operate freely, the tongue should feel very relaxed and loose in the mouth. Only the tip should be involved in the tonguing action: The faster the tongue is required to move, the shorter the distance it should travel and the lighter its action should be. A great many students unconsciously tense the tongue in attempting to develop velocity, and therefore lose all control.

The exact place on the tongue that should come in contact with the end of the reed will depend upon the individual and also on the particular style of tonguing desired at the moment. To say that everyone must tongue in exactly the same manner is failing to recognize that some may have different sized tongue and mouth formations. Each person must experiment to find which method is best for him. In general, the very tip of the tongue contacts the end of the reed quite directly for definite accents and the marcato style of tonguing as used in a sharp, brittle staccato. As the style of tonguing progresses from the sharp, definite sound to the soft, legato style, the part of the tongue used may shift to either the top of the tongue or just underneath the tip. At the same time, less and less of the reed will be touched by a continually lighter action of the tongue until, in the execution of the very softest legato, the tongue barely touches the reed at all.

One of the problems that most students have at this point is to try to separate the tonguing action from the breath support and the embouchure. The usual tendency is to increase or decrease the breath pressure with the change in tonguing style. The student must learn to keep the breath support constant, regardless of the action of the tongue. The action of the tongue will also interfere with the set of the embouchure. One of the worst possible habits is to tongue in a "chewing" fashion. The movement of the jaw and lips not only distorts the tone each time they move, but actually slows down the action of the tongue.

In working to correct these two errors, the student should practice in front of a mirror in order to observe any movement of the embouchure. Because breath and the embouchure must be under control before the tonguing problem can be solved, it is best to have the student concentrate on long, sustained passages and slurred exercises until these factors become automatic.

The attack is generally accomplished with the tongue, especially if a clean, definite starting of the tone is desired. The use of the word "attack" has misled some into thinking that the tongue must hit or strike the reed and that all notes must start with an explosive use of the breath. In view of this misunderstanding it would be better to use another word, such as "start," "begin," or "commence," in order to get away from the idea that the beginning of each tongued note must necessarily be forceful.

The tongue action in starting any tone is merely that of placing it gently against the tip of the reed and pulling it away quickly. At the same time, the breath pressure builds up behind the stopped reed. A proper attack is more a matter of preparation and timing of the entire tone-producing mechanism than anything else. The reed, of course, must be properly adjusted to respond instantly. In the very low register it is actually an aid in producing a good attack to drop the jaw slightly. This, however, is the only exception to the rule that the jaw or lip should not move other than in the very sharp, brittle staccato style of tonguing. When producing the sharp staccato, particularly at a rather slow tempo, it is almost impossible to keep the jaw motionless, but it should not be allowed to move excessively.

Although each tone is started with the tongue, a tone may be stopped with either the tongue (as in saying "tut") or with the breath (as in saying "tuh"). Not all notes which are marked staccato should be played with the "tut" style of tonguing. It should only be used in passages in which the composer seeks to use the rather humorous, dry effect of the bassoon's sharp staccato. Two quite typical examples are the bassoon solos in Beethoven's Symphony No. 4, First movement, measure 64, and in Dukas' Sorcerer's Apprentice.

All other notes which are marked staccato, marcato, and accent should be stopped with the breath, regardless of the length of the space between the notes. How much space should be allowed between detached notes will depend on the musical taste and experience of the student or teacher. Care must be taken in stopping the tone with the breath in slow tempi. Since it seems to be a natural tendency for a person to use the throat muscles and the glottis to stop the breath or to hold the breath in usual non-playing activities, this habit will have to be watched for in the untrained student. Closing the glottis and contracting the throat muscles invariably leads to a tense tongue as well as to faulty breath control. The breath should be controlled with the diaphragm and lower rib muscles only. The feeling will be one of suspended motion, rather than a complete relaxation of the breathing muscles. This feeling can be compared to the lifting of an object from the floor to a table; if the lifting motion is stopped several times along the way, the muscles are still tensed to keep the object from falling, but there is no upward motion. The teacher should pay particular attention to the embouchure during this type of tonguing to see that it is set before the tone starts and is not relaxed until after the tone is stopped. For a series of breath-stopped tones in a phrase, the embouchure should not be relaxed until a breath is taken at the end of the phrase. Relaxing the embouchure before the breath stops the tone will cause a disagreeable drop in the pitch.

One of the most disconcerting problems to the advanced bassoonist is how to develop a rapid and flexible tonguing facility. There is no doubt that some individuals can tongue naturally more rapidly than others, but most of those who are having trouble with a sluggish or an irregular tonguing technique may be having trouble in one or more of the following ways:

1. Poor tone quality in general due to faulty breathing and a closed, tense throat. The tight throat particularly will hinder the action of the tongue. Any improvements in these areas will usually improve the action of the tongue.

2. Improper embouchure. A tense lower jaw (indicated by a puckered chin) will keep the reed from responding freely. This excess tension will also interfere with the muscles of the tongue.

3. A poorly responding reed or instrument. A reed that will not staccato readily can be adjusted by either opening or closing the tip as the case may be, or by scraping lightly at the tip. (See Illust. 16.) Tonguing facility is very closely connected with the flexibility of the reed, but the inexperienced bassoonist may blame the tongue instead of the reed. At the same time, the condition of the instrument should be checked thoroughly for possible leaks and sluggish or improperly adjusted keys. An instrument that has even the slightest leak will not respond readily to either slurring or tonguing. This is espec-

ially true in the low register from F to low B♭ but it may also affect the rest of the range.

4. Poor rhythmic concept and lack of coordination between the tongue and fingers. When the student has a reasonable amount of talent, the trouble is usually a lack of attention to the rhythmic content of the phrase. Being able to sing the rhythm and articulation pattern has often been found to be of assistance to the student on any instrument. To sing the pattern, one will have to have the right concept in mind. The conception and feel of the rhythm must come before the execution. Many of the student's articulation problems are due not to a lack of skill in tonguing, but to faulty or irregular fingering technique.

5. Improper concept and style of tonguing. Some players seem to have the idea that rapid staccato passages are executed by separating each single note with the breath or tongue (as in saying "tuh" or "tut"), and that clarity is gained by striking the reed harder with the tongue. Nothing could be farther from the truth. Not only does this result in a very unpleasant sound, but superfluous motion actually slows the tongue down. The type of tonguing which should be used for rapid staccato passages is the same as for legato, portamento, or sostenuto tonguing. The breath pressure is continued throughout the entire phrase as in holding a long tone, and the tongue barely touches the reed. At a slow tempo this would sound like saying "ToooToooToooTooo" (some prefer to say "DoooDoooDoooDooo"). At a faster tempo, the sound would be like "ToToToTo-ToToToTo." All rapidly tongued passages are executed in this manner. The spacing, or staccato sound, is controlled by the cleanness and lightness of the attack on each note.

The question is frequently asked as to what is necessary for an adequate tonguing technique. In terms of speed of tongue action, the bassoonist should be able to produce a rapid and clean single tongue staccato series at a metronome marking of about 120 beats per minute, four notes per beat. This may vary, of course, with the individual. Some seem to be physically capable of more velocity than others. For the most part, speed is only possible through constant practice and a very relaxed tongue. There are very few passages written for bassoon that cannot be handled with single tonguing. If the tempo is beyond the capabilities of the bassoonist's single tongue speed, the use of the slur two, tongue two articulation works very well (♪♪♪♪). For an extended series of rapidly tongued notes in groups of four, slur two, tongue two, and then tongue four (♪♪♪♪ ♪♪♪♪). The insertion of the slurred group seems to give the tongue time to relax. In addition to being able to tongue rapidly, the advanced bassoonist will need to be able to produce any variety of tonguing from the shortest brittle staccato to the softest kind of legato.

Although a few professional bassoonists have been able to develop a usable double-tonguing technique, it is generally felt that for the average student the time spent in this direction could better be spent on developing a cleaner single-tongue technique. For those interested in the double tongue technique, there are two styles that have been used at speeds above 126 beats per minute.

The first style is similar to that used on brass instruments. The tongue action is "tu-ku" (some prefer "ti-ki"). The "tu" involves the tip of the tongue touching the reed; the "ku" is made with the back or middle of the tongue touching the roof of the mouth. Although some individuals are able to produce this very easily, most players will have to spend many hours of practice to develop any kind of controlled speed and coordination with the fingers.

The second style of double-tonguing is a flipping of the tongue rapidly up and down across the reed. Only the tip of the tongue is involved. One sound is made on the upward stroke and one sound on the downward stroke. It is rather hard on reeds, however, and often cuts the tip of the tongue if used too much. Some individuals have been able to coordinate this with the fingers into some fantastically fast staccato passages, but it is doubtful if it has much value in everyday use.

Fingering

The teacher will find that, next to the problems of the reed, the advanced bassoonist is most interested in learning more about fingerings. Although basic fingerings are given in most instruction books, very few young bassoonists have had the opportunity to learn the use of the alternate fingerings or the several special or auxiliary fingerings which are necessary for the adequate performance of the more advanced literature for bassoon. However, the teacher will also find that many students are hindered in their playing development by a lack of knowledge of the more basic aspects of bassoon fingerings: the use of the thumbs, the proper use of the pianissimo key, the half-hole, and the flick keys.

The teacher should be alert for signs of undue tension in the hands and arms, as this can be a great hindrance to the development of finger facility. It may be found that the hands, arms, or even the body position are at fault and must be corrected before any progress can be made. For instance, a student who is attempting to play the bassoon with a neck strap and no hand rest for the right hand will have much difficulty with the right thumb technique, in addition to having needless tension in the entire right arm and hand. The right thumb must be kept absolutely free and ready to manipulate the four keys on the back of the boot joint. The habit of using the right thumb to support the instrument at that point will not allow for facility. If the neck strap is to be used, a hand rest should be added to the instrument and adjusted at the right height to allow the thumb and fingers to work freely without stretching or being cramped. If this is not possible, the seat strap type of suspension is even better, in that it allows the right thumb complete freedom without the hand rest. In either case, the right hand and thumb facility will be improved considerably.

Similarly, the balance of the instrument may be such that it exerts an additional weight on the left hand. This may serve to tie up the left hand fingers and thumb. The signs of tension often are: the little fingers will be either held out straight or curled under; the fingers will not curve naturally or the hand will be stiff and appear strained and white around the knuckles; and the forearms will be tight and hard to the touch. The student, with the help of the teacher, should experiment with hand and arm position and with the suspension of the instrument to find the most relaxed position. Constant attention to playing with relaxed arms and hands will be necessary before a smooth and accurate finger technique can be attained. The teacher will also need to make sure that the instrument is in good repair. Particular attention should be directed to the adjustment of the articulated key mechanisms and the proper balancing and tensioning of the springs (see Part II).

The position and use of the left thumb are often misunderstood by young bassoonists. Although both thumbs are used more in bassoon playing than on any other instrument, the left thumb especially has more to do with a smooth technique than is realized. Having to operate from seven to nine different keys singly and in combination requires that the left thumb be trained to move in the most relaxed and efficient manner possible. The position of the bassoon should be adjusted so that the left wrist is not bent at too great an angle, as this will very definitely interfere with the movement of the thumb. In order to develop any kind of facility in the low register from low D to B♭ below the bass clef, the teacher should see that the student is using the left thumb in the following manner: (1) develop the habit of releasing the pianissimo key immediately when low E is played; (2) depress the low D and C keys with the first knuckle of the thumb and not with the tip; (3) depress the low B and B♭ keys by keeping the knuckle on the C key and bending the first joint down in a rolling action. (Students with so-called "double-jointed" fingers or thumbs will have great difficulty with developing any kind of facility on the bassoon.)

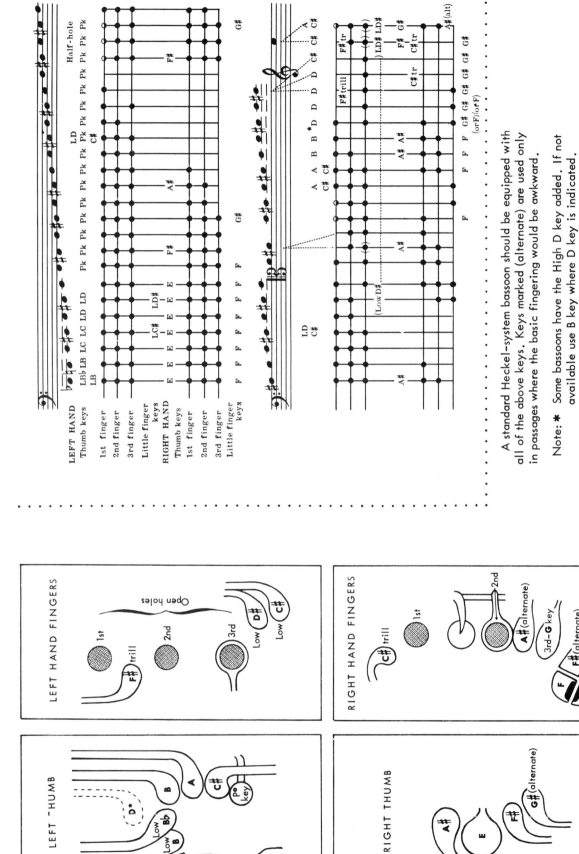

A standard Heckel-system bassoon should be equipped with all of the above keys. Keys marked (alternate) are used only in passages where the basic fingering would be awkward.

Note: ***** Some bassoons have the High D key added. If not available use B key where D key is indicated.
    o P-key – Pianissimo key, also known as Piano key or Crook key.
    L – Low; i.e. LB♭ is Low B♭ key.
    ( ) Key or hole is optional.

ILLUSTRATION 24

Chart of basic fingerings for Heckel system bassoon

The teacher should insist that the pianissimo key or crook key be used correctly. Because it is possible to play the bassoon in a rather rough manner without the proper use of this key, the student will often neglect it during his first few years of playing and will need constant reminders to use it until he becomes aware of its importance in artistic playing.

The pianissimo key is depressed with the left thumb in the playing of all notes from low F up to G♯ on the staff and for assuring a soft attack on high G and G♯ :

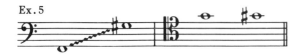

The use of the half-hole technique for the first finger in playing F♯ , G, and G♯ is similarly misunderstood by the inexperienced bassoonist, since these notes can be obtained by lifting the finger entirely off the hole:

The teacher should insist that these notes be fingered with the half-hole in the playing of legato, cantabile style passages, where particular importance is placed on the quality and intonation of these notes. The half-hole should also be used, along with the pianissimo key, for assuring a soft attack on the high G and G♯. It should be pointed out, however, that for rapid, technical passages the first finger can be taken completely off the hole. In this case, the slight difference in quality will not be noticed.

The notes of the second register of the bassoon (fourth space F♯ to D just above the staff) are fingered like the same notes an octave lower. While the overblowing of the octave of the F♯, G, and G♯ are aided by the half-hole technique described above, the bassoonist frequently experiences difficulty in getting the notes A to D to speak in passages involving a slur from another note, particularly if they are approached from the lower octave. Contrary to some opinions, the opening of the pianissimo key does not aid in breaking the air column like an octave key, although it must be open before these notes will speak clearly. It is therefore necessary that the student learn to use what are known as the flick-keys or flip-keys (Illust. 25) for slurring to either A, B♭, B, C, or D with any assurance. The C♯ and sometimes the

D require the use of a special fingering which is indicated in Illust. 27.

The flick-keys are to be found on the wing joint and are operated by the left thumb. The normal use of these keys is for the very high register notes for which they are named. The high D key is not found on the standard bassoon. The thumb action should be very light and should just barely flick the key with a sideward glance; it should not hold the key down. If the thumb is normally holding the pianissimo key down on the preceding note, it must be released just a split-second before it is necessary to touch the flick-keys. As a preliminary study the following exercise may be used:

The following examples are typical of the slurring problem made easier by the use of the flick keys:

★ Use the flick keys indicated above.

The advanced student will need to be acquainted with the use of both the regular and alternate fingerings for F♯, G♯, A♯, and D♯. Most bassoons are now equipped with rollers, which make the sliding between two keys much smoother. But for clean articulation, especially in slurring, it is imperative that the correct fingering combinations be used. The regular fingerings should be used in all cases except when the alternate fingering is needed to avoid sliding from one key to another with the same finger. In the following chart the regular or preferred fingering is given first (a), and the alternate is second (b).

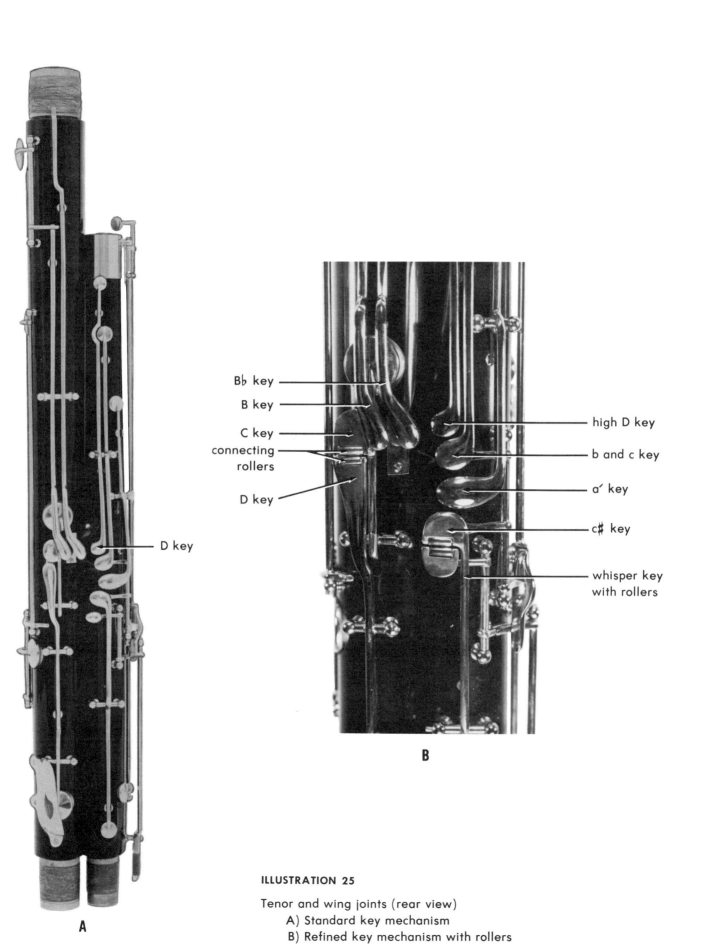

Bb key

B key

C key

connecting
rollers

D key

D key

high D key

b and c key

a′ key

c♯ key

whisper key
with rollers

A

B

ILLUSTRATION 25

Tenor and wing joints (rear view)
   A) Standard key mechanism
   B) Refined key mechanism with rollers

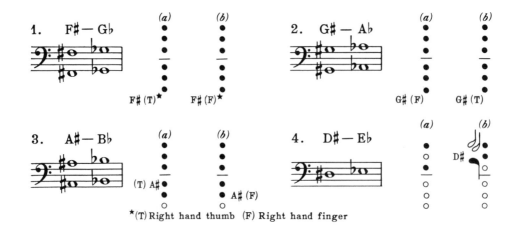

*(T) Right hand thumb (F) Right hand finger

ILLUSTRATION 26

Alternate fingerings

The regular fingering for F♯-G♭ should be used in all passages except when preceded or followed by A♯-B♭. In the following examples the proper fingerings are indicated by number and letter (e.g., 1-a, in Illust. 26.)

Ex. 10

Gordon Jacob, *Concerto for Bassoon**
Ex. 11

Gordon Jacob, *Concerto for Bassoon**
Ex. 12

*By permission of Joseph Williams Limited, London, copyright owners. (Sole selling agent Mills Music, New York).

While Examples 10 and 11 show the use of the alternate F♯-G♭ fingering, Example 12 shows the use of the regular fingerings for each of the notes involved.

When G♯ or A♭ is preceded or followed by F, it is necessary to use the alternate fingering, 2-b:

Ex. 13

Von Weber, *Concertino*
Ex. 14

A most interesting use of the regular and alternate F♯-G♭ and G♯-A♭ is given in the following example. The slur of an octave downward is generally most difficult on the bassoon, but switching fingerings helps with these two notes:

Ex. 15

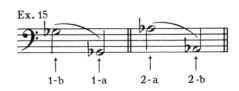

The alternate A♯-B♭ is used only for trills and for chromatic passages:

Ex. 16

There seems to be a misunderstanding among some bassoon players regarding the use of the forked fingering of D♯-E♭ as given in Illust. 26. A great many beginning players do not like to use it and seem to prefer the alternate because the forked fingering is out of tune and very sensitive to breath control and reed response. In the section on reed adjustment it was observed that one of the best checks or tests for a reed that is too stiff and hard in quality is this E♭. The reason that this fingering is not used is that the student is playing on a reed that is too stiff. A little working down of the lay will usually bring the fingering of the E♭ down to correct pitch and control.

The student who has a tight and constricted throat, along with poor breathing habits, will also have trouble with playing this fingering. It will be noticed that after these faults have been corrected, the forked fingering is much superior in tone and matches the quality of the surrounding notes more closely. The examples given in the next column are typical of passages made easier by the use of the regular fingering of E♭.

Ex. 17

Mozart, *First Bassoon Concerto*
Ex. 18

The alternate fingering for D♯-E♭ can be used for trills as indicated below:

Ex.19

In the following excerpt the alternate fingering is recommended because of the rapidity of the passage. The difference in quality is overbalanced by the cleaner articulation of the notes.

Piston, *Three Pieces for Flute, Clarinet, Bassoon* *
Allegro (♩ = 156)
Ex. 20

*By permission of Albert J. Andraud, Cincinnati, Ohio.

Since slurring to certain notes on the bassoon presents a problem for the advanced student, Illust. 27 presents a chart of special slur fingerings. These special slur fingerings should be tried only after the bassoonist is sure that (1) the regular fingering will not work, (2) he is using the correct fingering, and (3) the instrument and reed are in good working order. The teacher who is not a bassoonist will notice that most of the fingering problems are concerned with slurred notes in general and with certain notes which do not speak readily when approached either from above or below by a slur. All of the notes in question will respond if the student is allowed to use the tongue to break the air column. The difficulty begins in attempting to play with the more legato, singing style which is required of all instrumentalists.

If the particular passage confronting the player is actually impossible to finger or articulate by the use of the regular fingering, it then becomes necessary to find an alternate. In some cases where no alternate is possible, an auxiliary fingering may have to be used. These auxiliary fingerings are sometimes called "fake" or "false" fingerings.

Although the execution of very rapid technical passages is not the ultimate goal of the bassoonist, it sometimes becomes necessary.

Even the best prepared instrumentalist occasionally comes upon what would seem to be an impossible passage written for his instrument. In a case of this sort, the professional must look for a way to play it. This trial and error method usually results in the turning up of auxiliary, fake, or false fingerings. The young bassoonist should not take this to mean that any passage he cannot play adequately with the regular fingering should be tried with some other fingering: these are to be used only when all else fails.

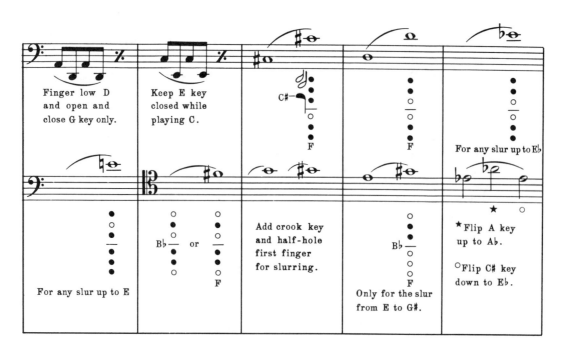

ILLUSTRATION 27

Additional slur fingerings

As a general rule, these auxiliary fingerings are based either on trill fingerings or harmonics of lower notes. The following two examples will illustrate this principle:

N. Ippolitow Iwanow, *Procession of the Sardar* from the *Caucasian Sketches*

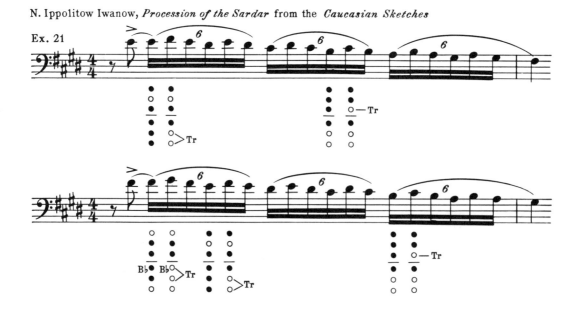

This well-known passage has baffled many bassonists. The use of the trill fingerings as indicated makes it much easier to execute cleanly.

The second example is a very difficult passage for the first bassoon in the third movement of Tschaikowsky's Symphony No. 5. Although this is not a solo, the bassoonist needs to be able to execute it with clarity:

Waltz, allegro moderato ($\quad\downarrow = 138$)

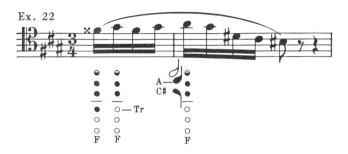

Ex. 22

The fingering for F× (G) is the regular fingering, while the G♯ and A are special trill fingerings.

In the performance of orchestral, ensemble, and especially solo literature, the advanced bassoonist will have occasion to use trills which do not usually appear on most available trill charts for the bassoon. These unusual trills are included in Illust. 28.

These trills are most often used by professional bassoonists, and will be effective on most standard Heckel system bassoons. Regular trills present no particular problem, since they are accomplished by merely fingering the notes indicated in the trill. There is one exception: the trill from A♭ to B♭ (G♯ to A♯). Although this is very seldom written for the bassoon, it does occasionally appear, and requires the addition of the A♭-B♭ trill key to the boot joint for anything like a clean trill. Trills on notes from low C down to B♭ are likewise very awkward and require a special technique called "wedging". For instance, a wedge or pencil is placed to hold the D key down to trill from low C to D. This procedure should be used only for special effects, however, as it can hardly be considered a legitimate fingering.

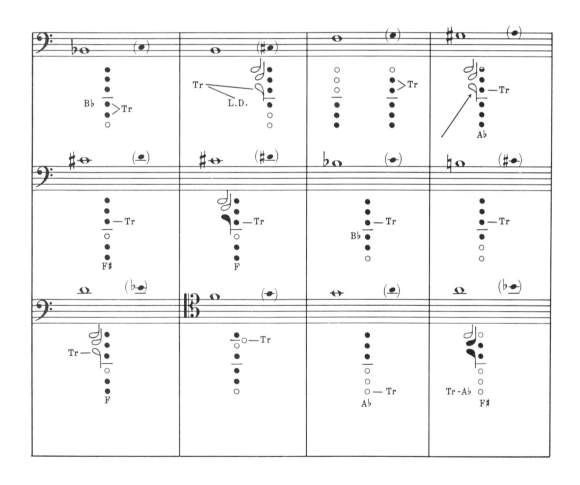

ILLUSTRATION 28

Special trill fingerings

63

Although the student bassoonist is usually most interested in developing greater agility in tonguing and fingering, the parts which he is called on to play often contain other problems which can be helped by a knowledge of special fingerings. The bassoon is frequently called upon to hold a very soft note over several measures. This ordinarily presents no problem to the player except for certain notes which tend to be rather difficult to control. By adding either fingers or keys to the original fingering, or by using a different fingering altogether, these notes not only become softer and darker in quality, but easier and less tiring to the lips. The following chart includes the notes which are the most troublesome in this respect:

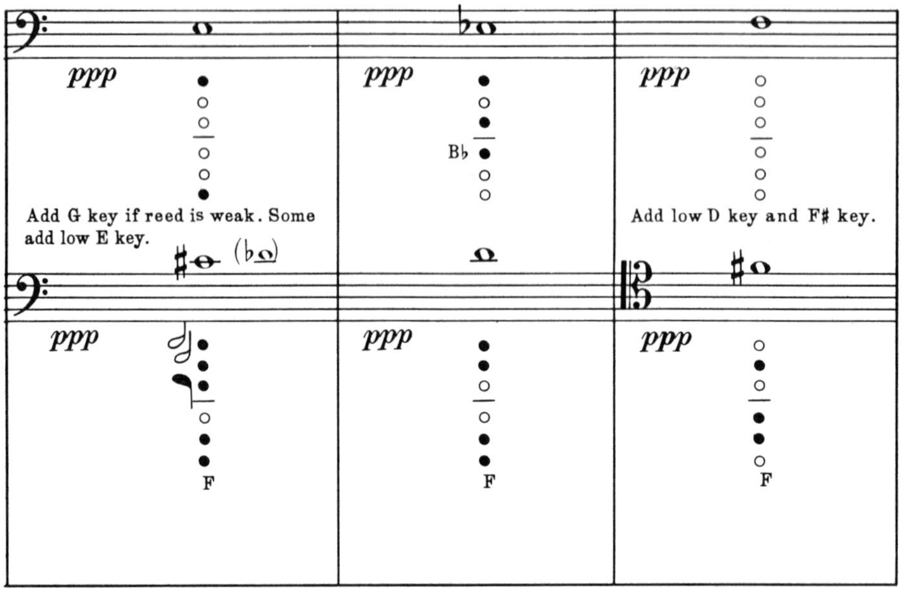

ILLUSTRATION 29

Fingerings for long tones

The additional and auxiliary fingerings which have been discussed here are not presented with the idea that every bassoon player will want to learn them or even have need for them. The bassoonist needs first to master the basic fingerings and the basic tonguing techniques. He will only need to refer to these special fingerings when a fingering or articulation problem arises that cannot be solved by the use of the regular fingerings and by diligent practice.

Combining Tonguing and Fingering

Many of the articulation problems at the advanced level are a result of faulty coordination of the fingers and the tongue. A large number of these mechanical problems are also due to a lack of concentration on the underlying beat and the lack of "feel" for the rhythmic pattern of each beat and the shape of the entire phrase. Too many students will play a piece, one note after the other, without any apparent thought as to its musical content. Time spent in the study of the rhythmic and harmonic structure of the music--by singing the melody and counting or clapping the rhythmic patterns--will often solve what seemed to be a problem of mechanical skill. If the student can sing the rhythm, he will usually be able to play it.

Failing to play the articulation as it is marked is another frequent problem. A lack of concentration on small details may account for at least a part of the general disregard for articulation markings. Or the student may not be able to play the music correctly because of a lack of development in fingering facility or because of poor fingering combinations. Often the student will have developed the habit of using the tongue or even the throat to cover up faulty finger coordination. This may occur in crossing the break (between fourth line F and fourth space Gb, G, or G♯) or between any of the notes which normally require alternate fingerings. The practice usually begins because of the difficulty of placing all the fingers down at once, but it will often remain as a habit even after fingering facility is improved. The breaking of this habit is imperative if the student is to play the music as written. Tonguing should be eliminated entirely for a time except for the initial attack, and all exercises, scales, chords, and difficult passages should be practiced slurred until the finger action is perfectly smooth and accurate. As the student develops a smooth slurring technique, he will learn that whereas he thought he had to tongue to cover incorrect or poorly coordinated fingerings, it is possible to slur them.

It often becomes necessary for the teacher to offer suggestions on how to work out difficult or stubborn passages and to discover which is at fault, the tongue or the fingers. The following rules of practice may be helpful:

1. Slur difficult passages at first, to direct attention to and make possible the elimination of fingering irregularities.

2. Practice tongued patterns on only one note to eliminate tonguing irregularities.

3. Practice very slowly and accurately. Gradually increase the tempo as facility improves, but practice no faster than you can play with good tone and accuracy of rhythm.

4. Concentrate on keeping the hands and arms relaxed as speed increases. Antagonistic tensions are usually the cause for finger irregularity.

5. Practice passages with grace notes, trills, turns, and other embellishments without the embellishment at first. After the basic rhythm and notes are well in hand, include the embellishments.

6. Pay particular attention to the notes which fall on the beat in very rapid passages. Although these notes may need to be stressed at first to establish the feeling of the beat and the rhythmic pattern, it should only be necessary to think the accent of the beat later in order to maintain the proper control of fingers and tongue.

PART V

Innovations

The composer Bruno Bartolozzi and the Italian bassoon virtuoso Sergio Penazzi have collaborated to create a new sonority, new concepts of tone production, and new notational signs in bassoon playing.

Reginald Smith Brindle describes the bassoon sonorities from Bartolozzi's "Concertazioni" for bassoon, strings, and percussion (Foro Italico, Rome) thus: "...such a gamut of unfamiliar sounds...that one can only describe as instrumental polyphony. Single sounds merge into chords, one pedal note is held while other notes emerge and coagulate in strange timbric agglomerations. There are extended passages in multi-note harmony—all these are made to merge into each other with apparent facility and simplicity." [1]

Composer Bartolozzi has written about some of these newly researched, tested, and prepared effects, including:

1. New fingerings for specific sound classifications, such as dark, open, light, or a combination of both closed and light.

2. New fingerings for quarter tones, creating new monophonic possibilities.

3. New fingerings for the performance of natural and artificial harmonics and/or combinations of one with the other.

4. New fingerings for performing "multiphonic" sounds.

5. New embouchure positions in order to alter and produce harmonic combinations. [2]

Don Christlieb has already succeeded in realizing some of these new sonorities and polyphonic effects. Composers Leonard Rosenmann and Barney Childs have worked with bassoonist Christlieb in preparing and composing the new music.

Innovations in Construction

1920   Rubber boot cap covering to prevent shock or damage to instrument.

1930s   Plateau C key, permitting swift action, eliminating key ring (not yet standard on all instruments).

1937   Lacquer, slightly elastic, to permit expansion and contraction of wood underneath.

1947   Sculptured one-piece "monolithic" keys.

1948   Taper design for swabs for better absorption of moisture from bore and finger tone holes.

1954   Reduced body size to accommodate smaller hands and to avoid finger-stretching by elementary and junior high pupils.

1955   Tuning slide for plastic school instruments.

1957   Rotary hinges instead of lever keys on tenor wing.

1959   Cork, or plastic tubes, preformed for easy replacement and adjustment.
Rhodium plate, tarnish-resistant metal plating.

1960   "Space Age" alloy and tempered keys for durability.

1965   Rocket wire springs that will not fatigue or rust.

1966   Snap lock to hold joints together; facilitates assembling and disassembling the instrument.

1967   Short bore bassoon ("American Symphony Orchestra" model).

1968   Tuning slide for bocal ("tuning crook slide").

---

[1] Reginald Smith Brindle, *The Musical Quarterly*, Vol. 52, No. 1 (Jan., 1966), p. 106.

[2] Bruno Bartolozzi, *New Sounds for Woodwinds*, trans. by Reginald Smith Brindle (Fair Lawn, N.J., Oxford University Press, 1967).

PART VI

Selected Literature and Discography

Bassoon teachers are constantly confronted with the problem of choosing solo and ensemble literature which is suitable for study and for contests recitals. The major portion of a student's repertoire is usually acquired from his teacher, whose acquaintance with the scope of available bassoon literature may or may not be adequate. Also the bassoon is too often thought of as an ensemble instrument only, and so the possibilities of the bassoon as an expressive solo medium have often been underestimated and neglected. In order to encourage the use of the bassoon as a solo instrument it is suggested that solo literature be used as study material instead of the usual etudes and other concocted studies. This is not to say that good technical studies and etudes which emphasize a particular technical pattern are to be eliminated. The student's practice time should be divided about

equally between technical studies, solo literature, and important passages from ensembles and symphonic works.

The aim of this section is to furnish a selection of methods, representative solos, and small ensembles with various other instruments by composers and teachers who have written serious music for the bassoon. Included also is an extensive bibliography of books and articles on various phases of the bassoon and bassoon playing written by many of the most widely known bassoon players and teachers.

The solos included are based on the following criteria: (1) to include a sampling of the wide variety of music available; (2) to offer a selection of music suitable for various levels of ability; (3) to present mainly music originally written for the bassoon; (4) to include examples of music that are worthwhile in themselves and interesting to study and perform.

METHODS AND MATERIALS

, J.S. *Studies from the Cantatas* (Bach). Hofmeister (Associated)

oni, U. *12 Studies*. Bongiovanni (Belwin)

h, M. *20 Etudes*. Leduc (Elkan-Vogel; Baron)

deau. *30 Etudes*. Leduc (Elkan-Vogel; M. Baron)

. *Grande méthode complète*. Leduc (Baron)

. *Recueil de Gammes et Arpeges*, tes 1 and 2. Leduc (M. Baron)

a, E. *15 Daily Exercises*. Elkan-Vogel 15 *Etudes journalières, Op. 64*. Leduc (M. Baron)

s, V. *Advanced Bassoon Studies*, . 32. Hofmeister (Associated)

emmes. *25 Etudes Polyphonique*. an-Vogel

n, G. *16 Variations*. Eschig sociated)

n & Pierne. *New Technique of the* Bassoon, Vol. 1 and 2. Elkan-Vogel

is, P. *12 Etudes*. Leduc (Elkan-el; M. Baron)

g, W. *48 Famous Studies*. Southern

nt, E. *Technical Studies, Op. 50*, parts. Leduc (M. Baron)

pieri, A. *Metodo progressivo*. rdi (Belwin)

. *16 Studi giornalieri di perfeziona-* to. Ricordi (Belwin)

er. *Le Débutant Bassoniste*. Leduc Baron)

, W. *30 Etudes*. Hofmeister ociated)

(Heckel System). *Chromatic Scale for Heckel Bassoon*. C. Fischer

Hendrickson. *Handy Manual Fingering Charts for Instrumentalists*. C. Fischer

Herfurth-Stuart. *Sounds of the Winds, Books 1 and 2*. C. Fischer

Jacobi, C. *6 Bassoon Studies, Op. 15*. Forberg (Peters)

____ . *Six Caprices* (Garfield). Cundy-Bettoney (C. Fischer); International

Jancourt, E. *26 Melodic Studies, Op. 15*. International

Kopprasch, C. *Sixty Studies for Bassoon, Vols. 1 and 2*. C. Fischer

____ . *60 Studies* (Kovar), Vols. 1 and 2. International

____ . *60 Etudes* (Seyffarth). Hofmeister (Associated)

Langey-Carl Fischer. *Tutor for Bassoon*. C. Fischer

Lentz, D. *Lentz Method, 2 volumes*. Belwin

Milde, L. *50 Concert Studies, Bks. 1 and 2*. Hofmeister (Associated)

____ . *25 Studies in Scales and Chords, Op. 24*. International; Hofmeister (Associated)

____ . *30 Concert Studies, Op. 26*, (Kovar), Vols. 1 and 2. International

Modess, O. *Chromatic Scale for the Heckel Bassoon*. C. Fischer

Orefici, A. *Bravoura Studies* (Arthur Weisberg). International

____ . *Melodic Studies* (Leonard Sharrow). International

____ . *Orchestral Studies, 10 volumes*. Hofmeister (Associated)

____ . *Studi Melodici*. Leduc (M. Baron)

Oubradous, F. *Enseignement complet du bassoon, in 3 books*. Leduc (M. Baron)

____ . *Preludes-Etudes after Cokken*. Elkan-Vogel

____ . *Exercises Complementaires Technique et Melodique*. Elkan-Vogel

____ . *Scales and Daily Exercises, 2 parts*. Elkan-Vogel

Pares, G. *Daily Exercises and Scales*. C. Fischer

Petrov, I. *Scale Studies* (Dherin). International

Piard, M. *Quatre-Vingt-Dix Etudes*. Braun (M. Baron)

____ . *16 Characteristic Studies*. International

Pivonka, K. *Rhythmic Etudes for Bassoon*. Bärenreiter

Prescott, G. *Prescott Technic System*. C. Fischer

Satzenhofer, J. *24 Studies* (Kovar). International

Siennicki, E. *Technical Growth for the Bassoonist*. Summy-Birchard Co.

Slama, A. *Sixty-Six Studies in All Keys*. Henri Elkan

____ . *66 Etudes* (Herrmann). Hofmeister (Associated)

Solobook for Bassoon (Wojciechowski). Simrock (Associated)

Stadio. *Orchestra Studies*. Ricordi (Belwin)

Strauss, R. *Orchestral Studies from Symphonic Works*. International

Taylor, H. *Twenty Melodic Studies*. C. Fischer

Vaulet, A. *20 Studies* (Voxman). Rubank

Vobaron, E. *Four Lessons and Seventeen*

Studies. Cundy-Bettoney (C. Fischer)

____ . *32 Celebrated Melodies for Trombone* (Bassoon). C. Fischer

____ . *34 Etudes*. Cundy-Bettoney (C. Fischer)

Voxman, H. and Gower, W. *Rubank Advanced Method for Bassoon*, Vol. 1. Rubank

Wagner, R. *Orchestral Studies*. International

Weissenborn, J. *Bassoon Studies, Op. 8*, Vol. I, for beginners, Vol. II, for advanced pupils. Peters

____ . *Bassoon Studies for Advanced Players*, Vol. 2. Cundy-Bettoney (C. Fischer)

____ . *Method for Bassoon*. Cundy-Bettoney (E.C. Schirmer)

____ . *Method for the Bassoon* (Schaefer). Hofmeister (Associated)

____ . *Practical Method for the Bassoon* (W.F. Ambrosio). C. Fischer

____ . *Practical School for Bassoon, New Edition* (Schaefer). Peters

____ . *Studies, Op. 8* (Kovar), Vols. I and II. International

LITERATURE
Bassoon Unaccompanied

Apostel, H. *Sonatina, Op. 19, No. 3*. Presser

Dherin, G. *16 Variations*. Associated

Gyring, E. *Arabesque*. Henri Elkan

Hartzell, E. *Monologue 3. Divertimento*. Doblinger (Associated)

Osborne, W. *Rhapsody*. Hinrichsen (Peters)

Schröder, H. *Music for Bassoon*. Lienau (Peters)

Bassoon Duets Unaccompanied

Almenraeder, K. *Two Duos, Op. 8*. Jack Spratt

Blume, O. *12 Duets*. Vols. I and II. International

Bozza, E. *Duettino*. Leduc (Elkan-Vogel; M. Baron)

Catelinet, P. *Suite in Miniature*. Peters

Caussinus. *Six Concert Duos, Op. 14*. Jack Spratt

Couperin, F. *Concert* (Bazelaire). Leduc (M. Baron)

Devienne, F. *Duos concertants* (from Op. 3). Kneusslin (Peters)

Glasenapp, K. *Duets* (works of Ozi, Krakamp, Almenraeder, and Küffner). Associated

Gotham Collection of Bassoon Duets (includes 2 Almenraeder, 2 Caussinus and 35 Mueller Duets). Jack Spratt

Kueffner, J. *24 Duets* (Dherin). International

Mozart, W. *Sonate* (Bazelaire). Leduc (M. Baron)

Mueller. *35 Duets*. Jack Spratt

Porret, J. *12 Easy Duos, Op. 648*. Wormerveer (Henri Elkan)

Satzenhofer, J. *24 Duets* (Kovar). International

Ticciati, N. *Variations on a Theme by Mozart*. Hinrichsen (Peters)

Tomasi, H. *Croquis*. Leduc (Elkan-Vogel; M. Baron)

Two Bassoons and Piano

Handel, G. *Sonata in G minor*. International

Three Bassoons

Bergt, A. *Trio*. Hofmeister (Associated)

Bozza, E. *Divertissements*. Leduc (Elkan-Vogel; M. Baron)

Haan, S. de. *Trio* (March, Waltz, Quasi Adagio). Hinrichsen (Peters)

Kummer, G.H. *24 Trios, Op. 11* and *Op. 13* (Glasenapp-Kart). Hofmeister (Associated)

Four Bassoons

Dubensky, A. *Prelude and Fugue*. Colombo (Belwin)

Holland, T. *Cortege*. Peters

Maxwell, C. *Idyls of Four Goblins*. Avant Music.

Prokofieff, S. *Humorous Scherzo, Op. 12, No. 9*. Forberg (Peters)

Bassoon and Piano

Abbiate, L. *Scherzino*. C. Fischer

Ameller, A. *Fagotin*. Hinrichsen (Peters)

Antoniotto, G. *Adagio et vivace* (Oubradous). Leduc (M. Baron)

Bach, J.C. *Bach for Bassoon* (Krane), 9 solos. Jack Spratt

——. *Concerto in B-flat* (Wojciechowski). Sikorski (Belwin)

——. *Concerto in E-flat* (Wojciechowski). Sikorski (Belwin)

——. *Siciliano* (BWV 1063) (Cazden). Jack Spratt

Baines, F. *Introduction and Hornpipe*. Schott (Associated)

Beach, B. *Introduction and Tarantella*. Henri Elkan

Beethoven, L. *Adagio from "Sonata Pathetique."* C. Fischer

——. *Adelaide*. C. Fischer

——. *Allegro from "Sonata Pathetique."* C. Fishcer

——. *Minuet* (Trinkaus). C. Fischer

——. *Sonate, Op. 17*. C. Fischer

Bennett, D. *Bassoonata*. Southern

Bergman, W. *Prelude and Fugue*. Schott (Associated)

Bitsch, M. *Concertino*. Leduc (Elkan-Vogel; M. Baron)

Blazhevich, V. *Concerto No. 5* (Garfield). International

Bloch, A. *Fantasie Variee*. C. Fischer

Boismortier, J. *Concerto in D* (Sharrow). International

Bond, C. *Concerto No. 6 in B♭* (G. Finzo-W. Waterhouse). Boosey & Hawkes

Bourdeau, E. *Premier Solo* (Dherin). *2nd Solo. 3rd Solo*. Leduc (Elkan-Vogel; M. Baron)

——. *Premier Solo* (Voxman). Rubank

——. *First Solo. Second Solo*. C. Fischer

Bozza, E. *Burlesque*. Leduc (Elkan-Vogel; M. Baron)

——. *Concertino*. Leduc (Elkan-Vogel; M. Baron)

——. *Fantaisie* (Le). Marks

——. *Fantaisie* (Concours Paris). Leduc (M. Baron)

——. *Récit, Sicilienne et Rondo*. Leduc (M. Baron)

Braga, F. *Toada*. C. Fischer

Bruns, V. *Concerto No. 2, Op. 15*. (Dherin). International

——. *Concerto No. 2*. Hofmeister (Associated)

Buonocini, G. *Aria* (C) (Parr). Hinrichsen (Peters)

Busser, H. *Cantilene et Rondeau*. Leduc (Elkan-Vogel; M. Baron)

——. *Concertino, Op. 80*. Leduc (M. Baron)

——. *Piece de Concours, Op. 66*. Leduc (M. Baron)

——. *Piece in C, Op. 45*. Leduc (M. Baron)

——. *Portuguesa, Op. 106*. Leduc

(M. Baron)

——. *Récit et Theme Varie, Op. 37*. Leduc (M. Baron)

——. *Recitative and Theme with Variations, Op. 37*. C. Fischer

Carissimi, O. *Heart Victorious* (Barnes). Jack Spratt

Cascarino, R. *Sonata*. Boosey & Hawkes

Cervetto, G. *Sicilienne*. Leduc (Elkan-Vogel)

Challan, H. *Fantaisie*. Leduc (Elkan-Vogel; M. Baron)

Cherepnine. *Esquisse, Op. 7*. Jack Spratt

Childs, B. *Sonata*. Tritone Press (Presser)

Contemporary French Recital Pieces, Album of six original pieces. Contents:
Bloch—*Drolleries*; Lavagne—*Steeplechase*; Ibert—*Carignane*; Bitsch—*Passepied*; Oubradous—*Divertissement*; Duclose—*Quadrille*. International

Corelli, A. *Adagio* (Giacomo Setaccioli). Ricordi (Belwin)

——. *Adagio in A minor* (Parr). Hinrichsen (Peters)

——. *Sonata in D minor*. International

Corrette, M. *Sonata, Op. 20, No. 2* (d). Willy Müller (Peters)

Danzi, F. *Concerto in F* (Münster). Leuckart (Associated)

David, F. *Concertino, Op. 4*. Simrock (Associated)

——. *Concertino, Op. 12* (Kovar). International

——. *Concertino, Op. 12* (Laube). C. Fischer

——. *Concertino, Op. 12* (Voxman). Rubank

Dillon, R. *Lament*. Boosey & Hawkes

Dubois, P. *Neuf pièces breves*. Choudens (Peters)

——. *Sérénades*. Leduc (Elkan-Vogel; M. Baron)

Duclos, R. *Fagottino*. Leduc (M. Baron)

——. *Trois Nocturnes* (Le). Marks; Leduc (M. Baron)

Dunhill, R. *Lyric Suite, Op. 96*. Boosey & Hawkes

Duport, L. *Romance*. Jack Spratt

Dutilleux, H. *Sarabande et Cortege* (Concours Paris). Leduc (M. Baron)

Dvorak, A. *Largo*, from "New World Symphony." C. Fischer

Eccles, H. *Sonata in G Minor* (Sharrow). International

Eder, H. *Sonatine, Op. 34, No. 3*. Doblinger (Associated)

Elgar, E. *Salut D'Amour* (Trinkaus). C. Fischer

——. *Theme* from "Pomp and Circumstance," Op. 39, No. 1 (Akers). C. Fischer

Etler, A. *Sonata*. Associated

Fasch, J. *Sonata in C*. Peters

Feld, J. *Concerto*. Leduc (Elkan-Vogel; M. Baron)

Flament, E. *Concert Piece, Op. 13*. C. Fischer

Fuchs, J. *Concerto in B-flat* (Gâbry-Sulyok). Schott (Associated)

Galliard, J. *Six Sonatas* (Weisberg) Vols. I and II. International

——. *Sonata No. 3* (F). Willy Müller (Peters)

Genzmer, H. *Introduction and Allegro*. Peters

Gliere, R. *Humoresque, Op. 35* (Kovar). International

——. *Impromptu, Op. 35* (Kovar). International

Godfrey. *Lucy Long*. C. Fischer

Gottwald. *Fantasie Heroique*. C. Fischer

Grafe, J. *Grand Concerto* (Laube). C. Fischer

Graun, J. *Concerto B-flat*. (Töttcher). Sikorski (Belwin)

Graupner, J. *Concerto in C* (Schroeder). Leuckart (Associated)

Grondahl, L. *Concerto*. Peters

Haan, S. de. *Scherzo*. Schott (Associated)

Handel, G. *Concerto in C minor*. Southern

——. *Sonata in G minor*. International

——. *Sound an Alarm* (Barnes), Jack Spratt

Hassler, H. *Andante and Rondo from Concerto* (Laube). C. Fischer

Haydn, J. *Andante from "Concerto."* Jack Spratt

Heinichen, J. *Sonata in D*. Peters

Hekster, W. *Music for Bassoon and Piano*. Donemus (Peters)

Hertel, J. *Concerto* (a). Peters

Hess, W. *7 Recital Pieces*: I—*Laendle Rondo, Pastorale, Capriccio*; II—*Reigen, Lied, Deutscher Tanz*. Hinrichsen (Peters)

Hindemith, P. *Sonata*. Schott (Associated)

Horder, M. *Hornpipe and Trio*. Hinrichsen (Peters)

Hummel, J. *Grand Concerto for Bassoon* (Tyree). Rubank

Ibert, J. *Arabesque* ("Carignane"). International

——. *Little White Mule, The*. Leduc (Elkan-Vogel)

Isaac, M. *Jolly Dutchman, The*. C. Fischer

Jacob, G. *Concerto*. J. Williams, London

Jancourt, E. *Reverie*. C. Fischer

Jeanjean, P. *Prelude et Scherzo*. Leduc (M. Baron)

Jolivet, A. *Concerto*. Heugel (Presser)

Kelkel, M. *Concerto for Bassoon and Orchestra, Op. 13* (Reduction for Bassoon and Piano). Editions Musicales Transatlantiques (Presser)

Kennaway, L. *Interrupted Serenade*. Peters

snar, M. *Clown Festival*. C. Fischer

___. *Gavotte*. C. Fischer

ghardt, A. *Romanze*. C. Fischer

esler, A. *Canzone*. Southern

epsch. *Down in a Deep Cellar* (argent). C. Fischer

kel. *Concertino*. C. Fischer

dowski. *Concerto*. Peters

tier. *Danse Bouffonne*. Leduc M. Baron)

om. *Lullaby* (Findlay). C. Fischer

el, J. *Burlesca*. Henri Elkan

vsky. *Happy Day, The*. C. Fischer

ganini, Q. *Rastus Ryan* (Negro ovelette). C. Fischer

cello, B. *Adagio and Allegro* (Merriman). Southern

. *Allegretto* (Oubradous). Leduc (Elkan-Vogel; M. Baron)

. *Largo and Allegro* (Merriman). outhern

. *Sonata in A minor* (Sharrow). ternational

. *Sonata in E minor* (Sharrow). ternational

. *Sonata in F Major*. International

. *Sonata in G minor*. International

teau. *Morceau Vivant* (Barnes). Jack ratt

telli, H. *Theme & Variations, Op. 74.* chig (Associated)

rat, E. *Petites Inventions, Op. 39,* o. 4. Eschig (Associated)

delssohn, F. *On Wings of Song* inkaus). C. Fischer

ci, L. *Sonata in G minor, Op. 3,* o. 4 (Bergmann). Schott (Associated)

le. *Mummers*. C. Fischer

lemans, A. *Rhapsody*. Henri Elkan

ser, E. *Concerto Oriental*. Jack Spratt

e, L. *Andante and Rondo*. C. Fischer

. *Tarantella, Op. 20.* International

shnikov, D. *Scherzo* (Dherin). ernational

tz, E. *Scherzo*. Zimmerman (Peters)

quet, J. *Ballade*. C. Fischer

art, W. *Concerto No. 1, Opus 96* flat), K. 191. Elkan-Vogel; Cundy-ttoney (C. Fischer)

. *Concerto in B-flat, K. 191* (Kling). ssociated)

. *Concerto No. 1, K. 191* (cadenzas G. Pierne and Ibert). Leduc Baron)

. *Concerto No. 1, K. 191* eissman). Boosey & Hawkes

. *Concerto in B-flat, K. 191* eisberg). International

. *Concerto No. 2* (B-flat) (Seiffert). ters

. *1st Bassoon Concerto, Op. 96, K.* (Moritz) with cadenzas. Jack Spratt

. *2nd Bassoon Concerto in Bb.* Jack ratt

Müthel, J. *Concerto in C* (Wollheim) Bote and Bock (Associated)

Offenbach, J. *La Musette* (Laube). C. Fischer

Neukomm. *Aria* (Kaplan). Jack Spratt

Pergolesi, G. *Canzona* (Barnes). Jack Spratt

Pfeiffer, F. *Concerto in B-flat* (Hennige). Leuckart (Associated)

Phillips, B. *Concert Piece*. C. Fischer

Pierné, G. *Concert Prelude, Op. 53.* Salabert (Belwin)

___. *Concertpiece, Op. 35* (Garfield). International

___. *Solo de Concert, Op. 35.* Leduc (M. Baron)

___. *Solo de Concert, Op. 35* (Voxman). Rubank

Presser, W. *Suite*. Tritone Press (Presser)

Reicha, A. *Sonata in B-flat* (Leber-mann). Schott (Associated)

Rhoads, W. *Ten Solos for Concert and Contest*. Southern

Rimsky-Korsakov, N. *Concerto* (Garfield). International

Rivier, J. *Concerto*. Salabert (Belwin)

Rössler-Rosetti, F. *Concerto in B-flat* (Stevens). Schott (Associated)

Rutherfranz, R. *Divertimento*. Henri Elkan

Saint-Saens, C. *Sonata for Bassoon and Piano, Op. 168.* Durand (Elkan-Vogel)

Sammartini, G. *Canzonetta* (Oubra-dous). Leduc (Elkan-Vogel; M. Baron)

Scarlatti, A. *Aria* from opera "Tigraine" (Barnes). Jack Spratt

Schaefer, A. *Capriccio*. Peters; Sikorski (Belwin)

Schiff, H. *4 Duos*. Doblinger (Associated)

Schoeck, O. *Sonata, Op. 41* (bn., cl.) Breitkopf & Härtel (Associated)

Schoenbach, S. (ed) *Solos for the Bassoon Player*. Boston Music Co.

Schollum, R. *Sonatina, Op. 55, No. 3.* Doblinger (Associated)

___. *Sonatina, Op. 57, No. 3.* Doblinger (Associated)

Schreck. *Sonate, Op. 9.* C. Fischer

Schubert, F. *Three Themes from Franz Schubert* (Isaac): 1—*Melody*; 2—*Lullaby*; 3—*The Rosamunde Air*. C. Fischer

Semler-Collery, J. *Recitative and Finale*. Eschig (Associated)

Senaille, J. *Allegro Spiritoso*. Southern

Smith, D.S. *Caprice*. C. Fischer

Spohr, L. *Adagio* (Wojciechowski). Simrock (Associated)

Stamitz, K. *Concerto in F* (Wojciechowski). Sikorski (Belwin)

___. *Double Concerto in B-flat for Clarinet, Bassoon and Piano* (Wojciechowski). Sikorski (Belwin)

Starokadomsky, M. *Four Pieces, Op. 25* (Dherin). International

Stevens, Halsey. *3 Pieces*. Peters

Stout, A. *Serenity, Op. 11* (Bsn and organ). Peters

Sukhanek. *Concertino* (Dherin). International

Tansman, A. *Sonatina*. Eschig (Associated)

___. *Suite*. Eschig (Associated)

Telemann, G. *Aria from "Pimpinone"* (Barnes). Jack Spratt

___. *Sonate in F minor* (Kovar). International

Tenaglia. *Aria* (f). Peters

Tschaikowsky, P. *Andante Cantabile*. C. Fischer

___. *Chant Sans Paroles* (Song Without Words) (Trinkaus). C. Fischer

___. *5 Pieces* (Kostlan). Hofmeister (Associated)

___. *Impromptu* (Seay). Jack Spratt

Ulrich. *Rondo Energico*. C. Fischer

Vanhal, J. *Concerto in C* (Schwamberger). Simrock (Associated)

Viola, A. *Concerto* (F). Heinrichshofen (Peters)

Vivaldi, A. *Concerto in A minor* (Ephrikian). Ricordi (Belwin)

___. *Concerto in A minor* (Sharrow). International

___. *Concerto in A minor, #2* (Ephrikian). Ricordi (Belwin)

___. *Concerto in B-flat, "La Notte"* (Ghedini). International

___. *Concerto in B-flat, "La Notte"* (Vene). Ricordi (Belwin)

___. *Concerto in D minor* (Weisberg). International

___. *Concerto in E minor* (Sharrow). International

___. *Concerto in F Major*. Colombo (Belwin)

___. *Concerto in G minor*. Ricordi (Belwin)

___. *Concerto in G minor, No. 11* (Smith/Kardt). Colombo (Belwin)

___. *Concerto in G minor, No. 23* (Smith). Colombo (Belwin)

___. *Sonata in A minor* (Garfield). International

___. *Sonata in E minor* (Weisberg). International

Vogel, J. *Concerto in C* (Wojciechowski). Sikorski (Belwin)

Weber, C.M. von. *Adagio from "Concerto, Op. 75."* C. Fischer

___. *Andante et Rondo Hongrois, Op. 35* (Flament). Leduc (M. Baron)

___. *Andante and Rondo Ongarese, Op. 35* (Kovar). International

___. *Concertino, Op. 26* (Kovar). International

___. *Concerto, Op. 75* (Schoenbach). Cundy-Bettoney (C. Fischer)

___. *Concerto in F, Op. 75.* Peters

___. *Concerto in F, Op. 75* (Sharrow). International

___. *Romanza Appassionata* (Laube). C. Fischer

___. *Rondo from "Concerto for Bassoon"* (Voxman). Rubank

___. *Ungarische Fantasie*. C. Fischer

Weinberger. *Sonatine*. C. Fischer

Weissenborn, J. *Adagio, Op. 9, No. 2.* C. Fischer

___. *Arioso and Humoresque*. C. Fischer

___. *Capriccio*. Cundy-Bettoney (C. Fischer)

___. *Capriccio, Op. 14* Hofmeister (Associated)

___. *Capriccio, Op. 14* (Dherin). International

___. *Nocturne, Op. 9, No. 4* (Dherin). International

___. *Romance, Op. 3* (Kovar). International

___. *Two Pieces, Op. 9* (Garfield). International

Wolf-Ferrari, E. *Suite-concertino in F, Op. 16.* Ricordi (Belwin)

Wright. *Episode Melancholique*. C. Fischer

Zbinden, J. *Ballade, Op. 33.* Breitkopf & Härtel (Associated)

Bassoon and Other Instruments

Amram, D. *Trio for Tenor Saxophone, Horn and Bassoon*. Peters

Bach, C.P.E. *Six Sonatas for Clarinet, Bassoon and Piano*. International

Bach, J.S. *Sinfonia in A minor* (Flute, Oboe, Bassoon). Mills

Beethoven, L. *Bagatelle, Op. 33, No. 2,* for Flute, Bb Clarinet (Oboe) and Bassoon (Elkan). Henri Elkan.

___. *Three Duos* (Clarinet and Bassoon). Associated

___. *Trio, Op. 38,* for Clarinet, Bassoon (Cello) and Piano. Musica Rara (Rubank)

___. *Trio in G Major* (Bassoon, Flute and Piano). International

Boismortier, J. *Concerto in A minor, "Zampogna"* (Ruf). Ricordi (Belwin)

___. *Sonata in E minor, Op. 37, No. 2,* for Flute (Oboe, Vn), Viola da gamba (Bn, Vc) and Basso Continuo (Ruf). Bärenreiter-Neuwerk

Bourguignon, F. de. *Suite, Op. 80* (for Oboe, Clarinet and Bassoon). Henri Elkan

Bove. *Petit Trio* (Bassoon, Clarinet and Oboe). C. Fischer

Bozza, E. *Suite Breve en Trio* (Oboe, Clarinet and Bassoon). Leduc (Elkan-Vogel; M. Baron).

Clementi. *Sonatina, Op. 36, No. 3* for Flute, Bb Clarinet (Oboe) and Bassoon (Elkan). Henri Elkan

Couperin, F. *Les Bacchanales,* for Flute, Bb Clarinet (Oboe) and Bassoon (Elkan). Henri Elkan

Danzi, F. *Quartet in B♭, Op. 40, No. 3,* for Bassoon and String Trio. Musica Rara (Rubank)

____. *Quintet in D Minor, Op. 41,* for Piano, Oboe, Clarinet, Horn, and Bassoon. Musica Rara (Rubank)

Devienne, F. *Quintet in C, Op. 73, No. 1,* for Bassoon and String Trio. Musica Rara (Rubank)

Dittersdorf, C. *Partia in D,* for 2 Oboes, 2 Horns and Bassoon. Musica Rara (Rubank)

Dussek. *Canzonetta for Flute, B♭ Clarinet (Oboe) and Bassoon* (Elkan). Henri Elkan

Dvorak, A. *Serenade in D Minor, Op. 44,* for 2 Oboes, 2 Clarinets, 2 Bassoons, Contrabassoon, 3 Horns, Cello and Bass. Musica Rara (Rubank)

Eisenmann, W. *Divertimento for 2 Clarinets in B♭ and Bassoon.* Sikorski (Belwin)

Fasch, J. *Sonata in F for 2 Oboes and Bassoon* (Wojciechowski). Sikorski (Belwin)

____. *Sonata (C) for Bassoon (Violoncello) and Piano* (Violoncello or viola da gamba ad lib). Peters

Francaix, J. *Divertissement* (for Bassoon, Clarinet & Oboe). Schott (Associated)

Gebauer, F. *6 Duos, Op. 8*—for Clarinet and Bassoon (Wojciechowski) Vol. 1; Vol. 2. Sikorski (Belwin)

Glinka, M. *Trio Pathetique,* for Clarinet, Bassoon (Cello) and Piano. Musica Rara (Rubank)

Grieg, E. *Rigaudon for Flute, B♭ Clarinet and Bassoon* (Elkan). Henri Elkan

Haan, S. de. *Divertimento for Bassoon and Clarinet.* Peters

Handel, G. *Fire Work Suite for Flute, B♭ Clarinet and Bassoon, or Flute, Oboe and Bassoon* (Elkan). Henri Elkan

____. *Fugue from 2nd Cello Sonata,* for Flute, B♭ Clarinet (Oboe) and Bassoon (Elkan). Henri Elkan

____. *Rigaudon, Bourrée and March,* for 2 Oboes and Bassoon with optional Side-Drum. Musica Rara (Rubank)

____. *Suite from "Music for the Royal Fireworks"* (David Stone). Novello

____. *Two Arias,* for 2 Oboes, 2 Horns and Bassoon. Musica Rara (Rubank)

Haydn, J. *Divertimento No. 2 in F (Parthia)* (Robbins Landon), 2 Oboes, 2 Bassoons, 2 Horns. Doblinger (Associated)

____. *Divertimento No. 3 in C (Feld-Parthie)* (Robbins Landon), 2 Oboes, 2 Bassoons, 2 Horns. Doblinger (Associated)

____. *Feldpartie in C,* for 2 Oboes, 2 Horns and 2 Bassoons. Musica Rara (Rubank)

____. *Octet (F),* 2 Oboes, 2 Clarinets, 2 Bassoons, 2 Horns. Peters

____. *Parthia in F* (Hoboken II:F:12). Musica Rara (Rubank)

____. *Three English Military Marches* (Hoboken VIII 1, 2 and 3), for Trumpet, 2 Horns, 2 Clarinets, 2 Bassoons, Serpent and Drums. Musica Rara (Rubank)

Höffer, P. *Theme with Variations*—for Oboe, Clarinet, Bassoon. Sikorski (Belwin)

Hovhaness, A. *Divertimento, Op. 61, No. 5* (Oboe, Clarinet, Horn and Bassoon). Peters

____. *Prelude and Fugue* (Oboe/Flute and Bassoon). Peters

____. *Suite (d), Op. 21,* for English Horn and Bassoon. Peters

____. *Suite, Op. 23,* for Oboe and Bassoon. Peters

Josten. *Trio* (Bassoon, Clarinet and Flute). Arrow

Jongen, J. *Trio* (Bassoon, Clarinet and Oboe). Andraud (Southern)

Keller, H. *Five Pieces for Bassoon and Clarinet.* Associated

Koutzen, B. *Music for Alto Saxophone, Bassoon and Cello.* Associated

Lybbert, D. *Trio for Winds* (Clarinet, Horn, Bassoon). Peters

Maasz, G. *Divertimento*—for Flute, Clarinet, and Bassoon. Sikorski (Belwin)

Maxwell, C. *Trio* (Flute, Bassoon and Horn). Southern

Mozart, W. *Adagio from "Sonatina No. 5" for Flute, B♭ Clarinet (Oboe), and Bassoon* (Elkan). Henri Elkan

____. *Alleluia,* for Flute, B♭ Clarinet (Oboe) and Bassoon (Elkan). Henri Elkan

____. *Cassazione* (Oboe or Flute, Clarinet, French Horn, Bassoon). Andraud (Southern)

____. *Quintet* (Oboe, Clarinet, French Horn, Bassoon and Piano), K. 452. Southern; Breitkopf & Härtel (Associated)

____. *Serenade No. 11 in E♭* K. 375, for 2 Oboes, 2 Clarinets, 2 Bassoons, 2 Horns. Breitkopf & Härtel (Associated)

____. *Sonata for Bassoon and Cello,* K. 292. Breitkopf & Härtel (Associated); Elkan-Vogel

Naumann, J. *Duet in B-flat*—for Oboe and Bassoon (Bormann). Sikorski (Belwin)

Perceval, J. *Serenata* (Bassoon, Clarinet and Flute). Southern (NY)

Pescetti. *Presto,* for Flute, B♭ Clarinet (Oboe), and Bassoon (Elkan). Henri Elkan

Piston, W. *3 Pieces* (Bassoon, Clarinet and Flute). Associated

Poulenc, F. *Sonata for Clarinet and Bassoon.* M. Baron

Sangriorgi, A. *Duo Sonata, Clarinet and Bassoon.* Colombo (Belwin)

____. *Duo Sonata, Oboe and Bassoon.* Colombo (Belwin)

Schoemaker, J. *Suite Champetre* for Oboe, Clarinet and Bassoon. Henri Elkan

Schütz, H. *Symphoniae sacrae, Nr. 3: In te, domine, speravi* (alto, violin, bassoon, basso continuo). Bärenreiter

Strauss, R. *Duet Concertino* (Clarinet, Bassoon and Piano). Boosey & Hawkes

Telemann, G. *Tafelmusik II* (Hinnenthal): *Quartet in D Minor* for 2 flutes (Oboes or Violins), Recorder (Bassoon) and Basso Continuo. Bärenreiter

Turechek. *Divertissement, F Minor* (Flute, Oboe, Clarinet, Bassoon). Witmark (Warner Bros.—7 Arts Music)

Van de Woestyne, D. *Divertimento* (for Oboe, Clarinet and Bassoon). Henri Elkan

Villa-Lobos, H. *Bachianas Brasileiras No. 6* (for Flute and Bassoon). Associated

____. *Trio for Oboe, Clarinet and Bassoon.* Eschig (Associated)

Weckmann, M. *Sonata a 4* (Oboe, Violin, Trombone, Bassoon and Continuo). Musica Rara (Rubank)

Zelenka, J. *Sonatas for Two Oboes* (Oboe and Violin), Bassoon and Basso Continuo (Schoenbaum): *Sonata I in F Major; Sonata II in G Minor; Sonata III in B-Flat Major; Sonata IV in G Minor; Sonata V in F Major; Sonata VI in C Minor.* Bärenreiter

RECORDINGS

Solos

Cascarino, R. *Sonata for Bassoon & Piano.* Schoenbach, bn; Columbia CMS 6421

Vivaldi, A. *Sonata No. 1 in B♭ for Bassoon & Continuo.* Hongne, bn; Epic BC-1344

Duets

Beethoven, L. *Duos (3) for Clarinet and Bassoon, G. 147.* Hongne, bn; Turnabout (3) 4076

____. ____. Hongne, bn; Vox SVBX-580

Mozart, W. *Sonata in B♭ for Cello & Bassoon, K. 292.* Finke, bn; Mace (S) 9080

____. Braun, bn; Deutsche Grammophon 138887

Poulenc, F. *Sonata for Clarinet & Bassoon.* Popkin, bn; Golden Crest (S) 4076

Villa-Lobos, H. *Bachianas Brasileiras No. 6, Flute & Bassoon.* Garfield, bn; Nonesuch 71030

Chamber Music and Ensembles

Auric, G. *Trio for Oboe, Clarinet & Bassoon.* Popkin, bn; Golden Crest (S) 4076

Beethoven, L. *Octet in E♭ for Winds, Op. 103.* Vienna Phil. Wind Group; Westminster 9008

____. *Quintet in E♭, Op. 16.* Philharmonia Och. Quintet (James, bn) Angel 35303

____. *Septet in E♭ for Strings and Winds, Op. 20.* Vienna Phil. Wind Group; Westminster 9711

____. ____. NBC Symphony; Victor 8000

____. *Sextet in E♭ for Winds.* Vienna Phil. Wind Group; Westminster 900[?]

Berger, A. *Wind Quartet.* Fairfield W[?] Ensemble; Columbia CML-4846

Carter, E. *Woodwind Quintet* (1949) Walt, bn; 3-Victor LSC-6167

Danzi, F. *Quartets (2) for Bassoon & Strings, Op. 40.* Grossman, bn; Lyrichord (7) 154

Dittersdorf, K. *Three Partitas for Win[?]* French Wind Quintet; Oiseau 5001

Glinka, M. *Trio Pathétique* (Clarinet Bassoon, & Piano). Oborin, bn; Monitor (S) 2068

Hill, E. *Sextet for Piano & Winds.* Ne[?] York Wind Quintet; Columbia CML-[?]

Milhaud, D. *Two Shetches for Woodw[?] Quintet.* New York Woodwind Quin[?] Counterpoint/Esoterics 505

Mouret, J. *Jeux olimpiques.* Wallez[?] Société Francaise Du Son 174130; 20130

Mozart, W. *Cassation for Oboe, Clar[?] Horn, Bassoon,* K. 452. Hongne, br[?] Oiseau 50016

____. *Divertimenti in B♭ for 2 Clarin[?] & Bassoon,* K. Anh. 229. Oehlberg[?] bn; 2-Westminster 9058/9

____. *Divertimenti, K. 213, 252, 253[?]* (Oboes, Horns, Bassoons). Vienna Wind Group; Westminster 9060

____. *Quintet in E♭ for Piano & Win[?]* K. 452. James, bn; Seraphim 6007[?]

____. ____. Philharmonic Orch.[?] Quintet; Angel 35303

____. *Sinfonia Concertante in E♭ fo[?]* Oboe, Clarinet, Bassoon, Horn & Strings, K. Anh. 9 (297b). Gehring Vox 1183

____. ____. Hongne, bn; Oiseau 50[?]

Poulenc, F. *Trio for Oboe, Bassoon [?] Piano.* Faisandier, bn; Angel S-36[?]

Schubert, F. *Octet, Op. 166.* Berlin Octet; Deutsche Grammophon 13[?]

____. ____. Vienna Octet; London 6051

Stravinsky, I. *Octet for Wind Instrum[?]* Columbia Symphony; Columbia ML-5672; MS-6272

emann, G. P. *Trio Sonata in E♭* Trumpet, bassoon & harpsichord); ennedat, bn; Philips WS S-9094

Ma-Lobos, H. *Trio for Oboe, Clarinet Bassoon.* New Art Wind Quintet; Vestminster 9071

der, A. *Quintets Nos. 3, 4, 6 for Winds.* New York Woodwind Quintet; on. Disc. 223

Concertos

h, J. C. *Concerto in B♭ for Bassoon.* enker, bn; Heliodor (S) 25056

. *Concerto in E♭ for Bassoon.* ukerman, bn; Turnabout 32478

art, W. *Concerto in B♭ for Bassoon,* 191. Bidlo, bn; Crossroads 22160168

. _____ . Brooke, bn; pitol (S) G-7201

. _____ . Garfield, bn; lumbia MS-6451

. _____ . Klepac, bn; liodor (S) 25002

. _____ . Oehlberger, bn; estminster 18287

. _____ . Sharrow, bn; tor LM-1030

. _____ . Zukerman, bn; rnabout (3) 4039

atti, A. *Concertato in D for Flute,* umpet, Bassoon and Strings. James, Vanguard 192

itz, K. *Concerto in F for Bassoon* d *Orchestra.* Zukerman, bn; rnabout (3) 4093

ldi, A. *Concerti for Bassoon &* chestra. Allard, bn; Counterpoint 08

_____ . Allard, bn; nesuch 71104

_____ . Bianchi, bn; nabout (3) 4025

_____ . Bianchi, bn; x (5) 10740

_____ . Klepac, bn; tsche Grammophon ARC-3116

_____ . Klepac, bn; Bach 70665

_____ . Schwartz, bn; yssey 32160012

Concerto for Flute, Bassoon & hestra, P. 342. Carmen, bn; yssey 32160012

_____ . Hoffman, bn; Bach 70665 *Concerti for Flute, Bassoon, Violin* Continuo. Hongne, bn; Epic BC-1344 *Concerti for Flute, Violin, Bassoon* embalo. Semprini, bn; Dover 5216 r, C. M. von. *Concerto in F for* soon *& Orchestra.* Zukerman, bn; nabout (3) 4039

Chamber Collections

Minus One: Beethoven, *Quintet,* s. 16; Mozart, *Quintet.* (Bassoon ing.) MMO-104

New York Woodwind Quintet: "French Encores"—Bozza, *Variations Sur Thème Libre;* Ibert, *Trois Pièces Breves;* Milhaud, *Madrigal et Pastorale;* Taffenel, *Quintette.* Counterpoint/ Esoterics 505; Everest 3092

PERIODICALS

Allard, Maurice. "Le Basson," *Musique et Radio,* Vol. 52 (November, 1962), p. 35.

Allison, Robert. "Two Improved Bassoons," *Woodwinds,* Vol. 6 (October, 1953), p. 7.

Almenraeder, Karl. "Making Bassoon Reeds," Part I, *Woodwinds,* Vol. 5 (January, 1953), p. 8; Part II, (February, 1953, p. 8; Part III, (March, 1953), p. 9.

Babin, Francois, "Improving Bassoon Fingering," *Woodwinds,* Vol. 5 (April, 1953), p. 4.

Bhosys, Waldemar. "The Reed Problem," *Woodwind Magazine,* Vol. 1 (December, 1948), p. 5.

Brindle, Reginald Smith. "The Current Chronicle—Italy," *Musical Quarterly,* Vol. 52 (January, 1966), pp. 106-9.

Brindley, Giles. "The Logical Bassoon," *Galpin Society Journal,* Vol. 21 (March, 1968), pp. 152-61.

Camden, Archie. "Archie Camden on Bassoon," *Composer,* Vol. 23 (Spring, 1957), p. 25.

Christlieb, Don. "A Treatise on the Manufacture of Bassoon Reeds," Part I, *Woodwind Magazine,* Vol. 1 (September, 1949), p. 6; Part II, (October, 1949), p. 7; Part III, (November, 1949), p. 7.

_____. "Measuring the Conical Bore of the Bassoon Emphasizing the Wing Joint: A Clinical Report," *Music Educators Journal,* Vol. 54 (April, 1968), pp. 71-3.

Cooper, Lewis Hugh. "Puchner Bassoon Factory," *Woodwind World,* Vol. 6, No. 2 (1964), p. 8.

Degan, Bruce N. "First Lessons on the Bassoon," *Holton Fanfare,* (December, 1961), p. 10.

Echols, Gary. "Solo and Ensemble Literature for Bassoon (Graded)," *The Instrumentalist,* Vol. 18 (September, 1963), pp. 91-3.

Eifert, Otto. "The Importance of the Bassoon Reed," *The Instrumentalist,* Vol. 18 (March, 1964), p. 52.

Figert, Peter. "The Continuing Bassoonist," *The Instrumentalist,* Vol. 22 (February, 1968), pp. 63-7.

Fitch, William D. "An Outline for the Teaching of Oboe and Bassoon," *The Instrumentalist,* Vol. 9 (December, 1944), p. 15.

Fox, Alan. "Defining the Two Types of Bassoons—Long and Short Bore," *The Instrumentalist,* Vol. 23 (November, 1968), pp. 53-4.

Fox, Hugo. "Factors to Consider in Buying a Bassoon," *The Instrumentalist,* Vol. 7 (March, 1953), p. 46.

Garfield, Bernard H. "The Ultimate Challenge for Bassoonists," *The Instrumentalist,* Vol. 19 (September, 1964), p. 59.

Gholz, Charles A. "Better Support for Bassoon Playing," *The Instrumentalist,* Vol. 8 (March, 1954), p. 36.

Groffy, Franz. "Piano-Key Mechanisms for the Bassoon," *Woodwinds,* Vol. 7 (April, 1955), p. 8.

Halfpenny, Eric. "The Earliest English Bassoon Tutor," *Galpin Society Journal,* Vol. 17 (February, 1964), pp. 103-5.

Heiss, John C. "Some Multiple-Sonorities for Flute, Oboe, Clarinet and Bassoon," *Perspectives of New Music,* Vol. 7 (Fall-Winter, 1968), pp. 136-42.

Hilton, Lewis B. "Articulation Problems of the Double Reeds," *The Instrumentalist,* Vol. 8 (May, 1954), p. 18.

Houser, Roy. "The Bassoon, an Enigma," *The Instrumentalist,* Vol. 10 (January, 1956), p. 38.

Jacobs, Arthur. "Passing Notes: Influence of A. Camden on Modern Bassoon," *The Gramaphone,* Vol. 40 (December, 1962), p. 313.

Jansen, Will. "From the Life and Work of Bassoon Players of the Past," *Crescendo,* Vol. 3 (September-October, 1953), p. 10.

Jennings, Vance S. "Woodwind Wisdom," *International Musician,* Vol. 62 (July, 1963), pp. 34-5.

Jones, Edwin W. "Those Bubbling, Blurting, Beautiful Bassoons," *The Instrumentalist,* Vol. 10 (April, 1956), p. 27.

Kitts, John S. "The Bassoon Bocal," *Woodwind World,* Vol. 8 (January-February, 1968), p. 10.

_____. "Meandering a la Bassoon Bocals," *Woodwind World,* Vol. 7 (April, 1967), p. 13.

Klitz, Brian Kent. "Some 17th-Century Sonatas for Bassoon," *Journal of the American Musicological Society,* Vol. 15, No. 2 (1962), pp. 199-205.

Kohan, Benjamin. "The History and Musicology of the Bassoon," Part I, *Woodwind Magazine,* Vol. 1 (January, 1949), p. 3; Part II, Vol. 1 (February, 1949), p. 4.

Kovar, Simon. "Simplifying the Bassoon," *Woodwinds,* Vol. 3 (November, 1950), p. 7.

Low, Floyd E. "Paul Bunyan, Bassoonist Extraordinary," *Woodwinds,* Vol. 3

(February, 1951), p. 10.

McClentic, Roger H. "Rental Bassoons? Why Not?" *Music Journal,* Vol. 26 (April, 1968), p. 42.

Malewski, Frank W. "Bassoon Bocals," *Woodwind World,* Vol. 7 (May-June, 1967), p. 7.

_____. "Double Trouble: Doctoring Double Reeds," *Woodwind World,* Vol. 7 (April, 1967), p. 4.

_____. "Double Trouble: Selecting New Reeds," *Woodwind World,* Vol. 7 (November-December, 1967), p. 7.

Marx, Josef. "The Truth About Vibrato, A Musicologist Views Its Development," *Woodwinds,* Vol. 4 (November, 1951), p. 4.

Meyer, Frederick. "Selected Books and Dissertations on the Double Reeds," *The Instrumentalist,* Vol. 22 (April, 1968), pp. 47-50.

Moyse, Marcel. "The Unsolvable Problem, Consideration on Flute Vibrato," *Woodwind Magazine,* Part I, Vol. 2 (March, 1950), p. 4; Part II, Vol. 2 (April, 1950), p. 5; Part III, Vol. 2 (May, 1950), p. 7.

"New Plastic Bassoon," *Woodwind World,* Vol. 3, No. 12 (1961), p. 4.

O'Connell, Thomas. "What Your Reed Can Do," *The Instrumentalist,* Vol. 23 (October, 1968), pp. 83-5.

Opperman, George. "The Vibrato Problem, The Seashore Study Applied," *Woodwind Magazine,* Part I, Vol. 2 (February, 1950), p. 5; Part II, Vol. 2 (March, 1950), p. 6.

Organ, Bob. "The Double Reed Family," (Three parts), *School Musician,* Vol. 38 (October, 1966), p. 22; (December, 1966), p. 12; (February, 1967), p. 14.

Palmer, Harold. "Bassoon Fundamentals," *The Instrumentalist,* Vol. 21 (January, 1967), pp. 50-2.

Patterson, John P. "Principles of Bassoon Tone Production," *Holton Fanfare,* (April, 1962), p. 7.

Peltier, Duane. "Reader's Comment: Bassoon," *Music Educators Journal,* Vol. 53 (April, 1967), p. 22.

Pence, Homer C. "Teacher's Guide to the Bassoon," *Woodwind World,* Vol. 7 (November-December, 1967), p. 22.

Pezzi, Vincent. "The Boehm Bassoon," *Woodwinds,* Vol. 3 (September, 1950), p. 8.

Polisi, William. "The Versatile Bassoon," *Music Journal,* Vol. 19 (February, 1961), p. 16.

Popkin, Mark. "Bassoon Reed Making, Maintenance, and Playing Procedures," *The Instrumentalist,* Vol. 21 (May, 1967), pp. 79-85.

Ruzek, Donald H. "The Contrabassoon," *The Instrumentalist,* Vol. 19 (January, 1965), pp. 48-50.

___ . "How to Make Your Own Contra-bassoon," *The Instrumentalist*, Vol. 21 (November, 1966), p. 45.

___ . "Adjusting the Bassoon Reed," *The Instrumentalist*, Vol. 20 (April, 1966), pp. 113-14.

___ . "Bassoon: The Clown of the Orchestra," *Music Journal*, Vol. 25 (April, 1967), pp. 34-5.

Schleiffer, Eric. "Adjusting the Bassoon Reed," *The Instrumentalist*, Vol. 22 (December, 1967), pp. 76-7.

___ . "The Bassoon: Three Technical Studies (Piano-Key Mechanisms, Bassoon Staccato, Speaker Keys), *Music Educators Journal*, Vol. 53 (January, 1967), pp. 57-9.

Schoenbach, Sol. "The Horrors of Bas-sooning, Casual Observations While Playing," *Woodwind Magazine*, Vol. 2 (February, 1950), p. 5.

Schwartz, Frank. "Dimensions of the Bassoon Reed," *Woodwind World*, Vol. 6, No. 1 (1964), p. 10.

Sharrow, Leonard. "The Bassoon is Archaic, The Need for a New Instru-ment," *Woodwind Magazine*, Part I, Vol. 2 (April, 1950), p. 4; Part II, Vol. 2 (May, 1950), p. 5.

Simpson, Wilbur. "Bassoon Reeds, How to Adjust and Trim Them," *The Instrumentalist*, Vol. 1 (November 1946), p. 5.

Spencer, William G. "Bassoon Vibrato," *The Instrumentalist*, Vol. 19 (February, 1965), p. 77.

___ . "Selecting and Adjusting the Bassoon Reed," *Woodwind World*, Vol. 4, No. 11 (1963), p. 5.

___ . "Forty Bassoons in Concert," *Woodwind World*, Vol. 5, No. 4 (1964), p. 12.

Swanson, Robert. "Pictorial Bassoon Fingerings," *Woodwinds*, Part I, Vol. 3 (April, 1951), p. 4; Part II, Vol. 3 (May, 1951), p. 5; Part III, Vol. 3 (June, 1951), p. 5; Part IV, Vol. 4 (September, 1951), p. 9; Part V, Vol. 4 (October, 1951), p. 7; Part VI, Vol.

4 (November, 1951), p. 8; Part VII, Vol. 4 (December, 1951), p. 9.

Waln, George E. "The Bassoon," *The Instrumentalist*, Vol. 1 (May, 1947), p. 11.

___ . "Playing Maturity Requires Train-ing and Careful Listening," *The Instrumentalist*, Vol. 11 (October, 1956), p. 30.

Walt, Sherman. "The Modern Bassoon-ist," *The Instrumentalist*, Vol. 4 (March, 1950), p. 18.

Washburn, Clinton Todd. "The Doubler's Dream (Uniform Fingering for All Woodwinds), *Woodwind World*, Vol. 4, No. 9 (1963), pp. 6-7.

Weidner, Robert W. "Bassooning With Recommendations for Reed Selection, Adaptation, and Preservation," *The Instrumentalist*, Vol. 18 (March, 1964), pp. 50-1.

West, Darle S. "The Bassoon and Its Reed: Some Practical Advice," *The Instrumentalist*, Vol. 15 (February, 1961), pp. 22-3.

Wilson, George H. "Bassoon Intonation: No Mystery," *The Instrumentalist*, Vol. 18 (February, 1964), pp. 65-6.

___ . "The Beginning Bassoonist," *The Instrumentalist*, Vol. 16 (May, 1962), pp. 67-9.

"Would I Make a Successful Bassoon Student?" *Woodwind World*, Vol. 7 (February, 1967), pp. 4-5.

DOCTORAL DISSERTATIONS

Bartlett, Loren Wayne. "A Survey and Checklist of Representative Eighteenth-Century Concertos and Sonatas for Bassoon." Ph.D. dissertation, State University of Iowa, 1961.

Bigham, William Marvin, Jr., "A Com-parison of Two Response Modes in Learning Woodwind Fingerings by Programmed Text." Ph.D. dissertation, Florida State University, 1965.

Dalby, Max Foreman. "Psychology and Method in Teaching Woodwind Instru-ments." Ed.D. dissertation, Utah State University, 1961.

Dominik, William Carl. "The Training, Experience, and Present Position of the Woodwind Instructor in Higher Educa-tion." D.M.A. dissertation, University of Southern California, 1964.

Klitz, Brian Kent. "Solo Sonatas, Trio Sonatas, and Duos for Bassoon Before 1750." Ph.D. dissertation, University of North Carolina, 1961.

Lehmann, Paul Robert. "The Harmonic Structure of the Tone of the Bassoon." Ph.D. dissertation, University of Michigan, 1962.

Lewis, Edgar Jay, Jr. "The Use of Wind Instruments in Seventeenth-Century Instrumental Music." Ph.D. disserta-tion, University of Wisconsin, 1964.

Merriman, Lyle Clinton. "Solos for Unaccompanied Woodwind Instru-ments: A Checklist of Published Works and Study of Representative Ex-amples." Ph.D. dissertation, State University of Iowa, 1963.

Spencer, William Gilbert. "The Teaching of the Bassoon in the High School and College." Ed.D. dissertation, Col-umbia University, 1958.

Teuber, Fred William. "Music for Wind and Percussion Instruments." Ph.D. dissertation, State University of Iowa, 1963.

Warner, Thomas Everett. "Indications of Performance Practice in Woodwind Instruction Books of the Seventeenth and Eighteenth Centuries." Ph.D. dissertation, New York University, 1964.

BOOKS

Baines, Anthony. *Woodwind Instruments and Their History*, rev. ed. New York: W. W. Norton & Co., 1963.

Bartolozzi, Bruno. *New Sounds for Woodwinds*. Translated and edited by

Reginald S. Brindle. New York: Oxfor University Press, 1967.

Camden, Archie. *Bassoon Technique*. London: Oxford University Press, 196

Carse, Adam. *Musical Wind Instrumen* New York: Da Capo Press, 1965.

Christlieb, Don. *Notes on the Bassoon Reed: Machinery, Measurement Ana sis*, rev. ed. (By the Author, 1966).

___ . *Pictorial Fingerings for the Bas-soon*. (By the Author, 1967; revised 1969).

Langwill, Lyndesay G. *The Bassoon a Contrabassoon*. New York: W. W. Norton & Co., 1965.

Lehman, Paul Robert. *The Harmonic Structure of the Tone of the Basso* Seattle: Berdon, 1965.

Leidig, V. F. *Contemporary Woodwir Technique*. Hollywood: Highland Music, 1960.

Rasmussen, Mary, and Mattran, Don *A Teacher's Guide to the Literature of Woodwind Instruments*. Durham N. H.: Brass and Woodwind Quarte 1966.

Risdon, Howard. *Musical Literature f the Bassoon: A Compilation of Mu for the Bassoon as an Instrument i Ensemble*. Seattle: Berdon, 1963.

Sawhill, Clarence, and McGarrity, Bertram. *Playing and Teaching W wind Instruments*. Englewood Clif N. J.: Prentice-Hall, 1962.

Thornton, James. *Woodwind Handbc* Albuquerque: New Mexico Univer Press, 1960.

Timm, Everett L. *Woodwinds: Perfor mance and Instructional Techniqu* Boston: Allyn & Bacon, Inc. 1964.

Warner, Thomas E. *An Annotated B graphy of Woodwind Instruction Bc 1600-1830*. Detroit: Information C dinators, 1967.

Weerts, R. K. *Handbook for Woodwi* Kirksville, Mo.: Simpson, 1966.

Westphal, Frederick W. *Guide to Te ing Woodwinds*. Dubuque: Wm. C Brown Co., 1962.